I WAS NEVER ALONE

Story by La Shawn Butler
Written by Joelle Valente

authorHOUSE®

AuthorHouse™
1663 Liberty Drive
Bloomington, IN 47403
www.authorhouse.com
Phone: 1-800-839-8640

First published by AuthorHouse 06/29/2011

ISBN: 978-1-4634-0604-2 (ebk)
ISBN: 978-1-4634-0605-9 (hc)
ISBN: 978-1-4634-0606-6 (sc)

Library of Congress Control Number: 2011907948

Printed in the United States of America

Any people depicted in stock imagery provided by Thinkstock are models,
and such images are being used for illustrative purposes only.
Certain stock imagery © Thinkstock.

This book is printed on acid-free paper.

Acknowledgements

First and foremost, I would like to thank God for all the blessings which He has bestowed upon me, for never leaving me or giving up on me, even when I wanted to give up on myself.

To me, it's been a long and treacherous journey, but we somehow managed to maintain. I know that the darkest moments made us want to give up, but we didn't. For that I am eternally grateful. God was with us every step of the way. Let's continue to pray.

To my husband John, I would like to thank you for your patience, caring, love, and for being as understanding as you are. You are truly a beautiful man. I thank God for bringing you into my life. You are my rock.

I would like to thank my five amazing children; Shawn, John Jr., Jason, Jasmine, and Jordyn. Thank you for being the best children a mother can ask for. Each and every one of you has your own space in my heart that could never be replaced. You give me a reason to be the best that I can be. To my littlest angel Jasmine, I will never forget your little cry. I loved you, but God loved and wanted you more. I know that you are looking down on all of us. I promise you that I will have another chance to hold you in Heaven.

I would like to thank my Mother-in-Law, Gloria, for all those Sunday dinners, and my Father-in-Law John, for being a friend and listening to me when I need someone to talk to. I love you both very much. You have really shown me the meaning of **family**. Thank you for welcoming me into your family with open arms.

To my Baby Sister, Diane, who I call Dee, we both have been through so much. We were separated for awhile as children, but I think it only made us appreciate each other more as adults. I still feel that protective instinct I had for you when we were little girls. I love you with all of my heart and soul.

To Sophia, I would like to thank you for always being there to support and encourage me every step of the way. Thank you for believing in me. You are more than my best friend, you are a sister to me.

To Authorhouse, thank you for the opportunity to publish this book. I truly appreciate your guidance, faith, and the detail you took to make my book become a reality.

To my dear friend and sister in Christ, Joelle Valente, I would like to thank you for all of your love and support. Thank you for now being a part of my life, my heart, and my family. Sis, you are not alone either. A special thank you to Marley Mariposa for designing my front & book cover. You realized my vision and for that I am truly grateful.

Dedication

I would like to dedicate this book to my father Gary Watkins. Dad, I can recall a time when you did not believe in God, but now every time I talk to you, I feel His presence. I don't know why you are still going through what you are going through. I just pray that it will be over soon. I am so proud of the father and grandfather you have become. I am so proud of your accomplishments even in the worst situations. Keep your head up, because you are not alone. I love you, Dad.

I would also like to dedicate this book to myself, my Soul mate John, my children; Shawn, John Jr., Jason, Jasmine, and Jordyn. I love you all and thank you for being there for me through the ups and downs. For loving me when I was weak and strong and for your patience when I ran out of my own. To baby Jasmine, you are now the angel in my sky. I know I will hold you again when I get to Heaven, but until then, watch over me. Mommy loves all of you. Oh, Lord, don't make me cry!!!

A special thank you to Sharlene Falls, award winning writer and film producer out of Atlanta. Thank you for believing in me when I was first starting out my acting career. You took a chance on me even though you didn't know me and were instrumental in me gaining the confidence to act and accept acting roles. You are now a part of my family and I am grateful to be a part of yours.

Table of Contents

Chapter One
The beginning…

Hi, I'm Lala and I was born in the inner city of Baltimore, Maryland, to teenage parents, Vienna and Gary, during the summer of 1970. I remember my mother saying it was the hottest day of the year. Since I was born a day after her due date, she predicted that I was going to be a fireball, because she spent so many hours in pain. She said it was the worse pain she had ever felt in her life.

She laughed when she recalled that when the doctors handed me to her that my eyes were wide open and I had a big smile on my tiny face. Two years later, my little sister, Diane, was born. I called her Dee, for short. By the time I was five and Dee was three, my mom had us living in a high-rise Housing Project in Baltimore. My dad was now in prison. Our two bedroom apartment was bare. We only had two twin mattresses in my room and a large mattress in Mom's room. She said she was trying to save money for furniture, which is why she had to work so hard.

Mom would leave us alone almost every night. Many nights, we had no food to eat. So, we would go to the High Rise across the street to my Aunt Nilsa's apartment and have dinner there. With my mom's constant absence, I had no choice but to take on the role of mother to my baby sister Dee. It was like having a real little doll that needed me. Dee never went to Mom for anything. She would always come to me to feed her, clothe her, bathe her, and play with her.

One night, my Mom went out, leaving us alone longer than usual. Again, there was no food in the house. It was really cold out, because it had just snowed three days earlier. So, I decided to dress Dee and myself. We headed out the door and started looking for our Mom. We walked around trying to find her and it was now two am in the morning. After

1

miles and miles of walking, we finally found her. She was outside of a bar crying, because her boyfriend found her dancing in the bar and beat her up. When she looked up, she was so surprised to see us. She yelled, "what's wrong?" Dee started crying and one of the ladies from the bar came to console her. Mom couldn't take it and went into the phone booth to call her sister Sharon. I overheard her telling Aunt Sharon that she couldn't take being a mother anymore. She said she just couldn't handle the pressure any longer.

Aunt Sharon came to pick us up. Mom's lip was cut, so Aunt Sharon took her to the Church Hospital on the East side of Baltimore. She needed six stitches. Although Mom had that cut on her mouth, she was still one the most beautiful women I had ever seen. She had a caramel complexion, long curly black hair, and a body that should have graced the front covers of magazines.

When Mom walked down the street, horns would go off and men would whistle. She always got attention for her looks. She attracted men of all colors. She was a natural beauty. I always thought she didn't even need make-up. That's why her boyfriend was so jealous and hardly wanted her to go out. Something she continually ignored and did anyway.

Vienna had experienced a lot of disappointments in her life. After her father Hank died, she met Gary and fell madly in love. They were high school sweethearts. Soon after graduating from high school, Vienna got pregnant with me.

A short time after my birth, Gary got arrested. He had been accused of attempted murder and attempted robbery. An eyewitness stated that she had seen Gary running down the street the same night that the liquor store was robbed. The liquor store owner was shot and killed instantly.

At the time, Gary was only seventeen. His neighbors came to know him as a drug addict and a thief, but not as a violent man. Gary was then arrested, picked out of a line up from the female eyewitness, and charged with murder. He was later convicted of first degree murder and sentenced to life in prison without the possibility of parole. There was no physical evidence and no weapon was ever found. Just one white woman who said she was walking down the street when she saw a black man running past her. Whom she later identified as Gary.

Since my dad always defended his innocence, he took the initiative to fight for what was right. So, he filed an appeal with a higher court and two years later, in 1972, it paid off. Gary was out on bail awaiting a new trial!! He then decided to take Vienna and Lala to Detroit, Michigan. He knew the risk he was undertaking, but he just wanted to get out of there. He was not allowed to leave the state. So, by doing so, he now was in violation of his parole. Gary was petrified, but he did it anyway. He figured he owed us a new start. My mom, Vienna, would've followed him to the Moon if she had to. She loved Gary so much and she wasn't about to let go. "Gary, you know we can't do this like this, said Vienna." To which Gary replied, "Vienna, don't question what I do, let's just go!" Vienna was nervous and unsure and wanted to talk him out of it, but it was no use. We were there already and it was done.

Two months later, we were forced to return to Baltimore. For two major reasons. One, I had developed pneumonia and spent several weeks in ICU and two, Gary learned that his mother, Betty was diagnosed and dying of colon cancer. "Gary, I also need to tell you something, said Vienna." "What now, Vienna, said Gary, what now?" "Ok, Gary, it's a surprise," urged Vienna!! At which point I heard her scream, "I'm pregnant!!" There was silence for a few moments. Then Gary, seemingly shocked and dismayed, replied, "oh, you are?!" Vienna knew it was the worst timing and with everything going on Gary was already too overwhelmed.

Gary decided to ask Vienna to marry him. "Uh, Vienna, listen, maybe we should get married and all," a doubtful Gary said. Vienna's eyes lit up like Christmas Trees and she started jumping up and down. That was the biggest smile I've ever seen my mother have in all my life! Vienna then preceded to inform the entire family!!!

At the time, Vienna was working at The Coffee Pot as a waitress. She didn't make much money. So, she relied on her tips to save the money to buy a wedding dress. She figured a cream colored dress would be appropriate since she already had a daughter, Lala, with Gary and because she was also pregnant with her second Baby girl, Diane. She also bought matching beige colored shoes. She then decided to buy Lala a little beige colored dress to match hers. Now, Vienna was ready to get married to Gary. The man of her dreams.

On Mom's wedding day, everything was chaotic. She was holding me on her hip and she looked at me and smiled. She said, "Lala, today, Mommy and Daddy are getting married." I didn't really know what Mom was saying and smiled, because she was smiling at me. Vienna's brother, Kevin, grabbed his car keys and we headed to my Grandma Louise's house, where my dad, Gary was living. They had planned to go to the Baltimore City Courthouse, but when we got there, Gary wasn't dressed. He pulled Vienna to the side and said, "Vienna, I know I said we should get married, but I'm not ready to get married yet." Vienna collapsed on the bed and started crying. "Gary, everything is ready, we invited so many people, what are they going to say?"

"Vienna, I want to be fair to you, but I'm scared." Vienna sat up in bed and took a good look at Gary. She knew just then he was right, but she didn't want to face the family with this news. Maybe Gary was scared now and Vienna thought she could talk him into it. So, she tried again. "Gary, I'm pregnant with our second child, I want you to be my husband and not just a boyfriend." Gary fell more silent and then walked away. Vienna felt like someone had taken a knife and jabbed it into her chest and just kept twisting. She collapsed on the bed again and began sobbing uncontrollably. She kept saying over and over, "how can you do this to us!!!" She was really crushed.

It happened to be pouring rain outside and Mom reached down, grabbed me into her arms and ran to Grandma's as fast as she could. It was two blocks away and Vienna couldn't get there fast enough. We were soaking wet when we got there. Vienna started crying again. Grandma Louis reached over and took me out of her arms. She knew Mom was in a lot of pain. Mom couldn't shake the disappointment off, so she went down into the basement where her older brother Ronnie was living. Ronnie, who was a heavy drug user and drinker, offered Vienna heroin for the first time. Vienna hesitated at first, but she wanted to end the pain and started taking the heroin.

She began to feel that taking the heroin would definitely take all her pain away. She felt so guilty, because she was pregnant, but her heart was hurting so bad, that she kept shooting up heroin to dull the pain. Vienna refused to talk to or look at Gary for several weeks.

She really didn't want to show her face anywhere anymore.

One month later, Gary was arrested for violating his parole by leaving the state. Back in the seventies, black men were severely scrutinized for their crimes. So, Dad was sent to jail and convicted for first degree murder. Vienna was devastated. She knew then that there would never be a chance for her happiness. She was pregnant again, alone, and really petrified. She also knew that black men were getting severe and unfair sentences, which made their chance at a better life quite grim.

Three months later, my grandmother Louise, passed away from colon cancer.

Back in the 1970's, if someone in your immediate family died, you were allowed to attend the funeral. So, They bought my father Gary in handcuffs and chained ankles. The family was so distraught about that. When my mother, Vienna, saw him in those chains, she broke out in tears and tripped up the stairs. She said, "dear God, why are you doing this to me?" She got silent and began to cry even more.

Several months later, in October, Vienna gave birth to her second baby girl, Dee. Dee looked a lot like me, but just smaller. I decided that she was going to be my live baby doll and that's exactly what she became. She adored me and followed me everywhere. You'd think I was loaded with candy canes the way she lagged behind me!! She always felt safest with me better than anyone else. First time I saw her, she just smiled and smiled like she knew who I was or something. We were inseparable after that. My mom would always bring other men to the house and introduce them as our "uncles."

"Lala, come here and meet your "Uncle Larry." So, I said, "Hi, Uncle Larry, I'm Lala and this is Dee. My baby sister." I knew he wasn't our "uncle," 'cause I never saw him before, but I played along so mom wouldn't feel embarrassed. I was so mature for my age. I took Dee's hand and walked her to our room so that they could be alone. I would cover Dee's ears when they got too wild. I could hear mom through the walls. All I'd hear was, "give it to me, daddy!" over and over again.

Made me wonder what he was giving her, but I didn't want to ask. Mom had a bad temper. She was always slapping me in the face if she didn't like something I asked her. So, I learned to not to ask too many questions. Unless it was something really important and I really wanted to know. One day, about a week later, she bought another "uncle" over and walked right past us into the bathroom. I brought Dee to the living room and sat her in front of the T.V. and then I ran and put my ear to the door. I was eager to hear what she said this time.

I could hear them talking about the drugs they had and that they were happy to get high together. After they took a few hits of drugs, then came the sex. Mom was so loud that I didn't even have to put my ear to the door anymore. I sat in front of the door and listened. "Yeah, baby, right there. Give it to me, daddy!" Oh, Lord. Why does she keep calling every "uncle" daddy?!! Doesn't she remember their names?! I started to giggle.

Just then, Dee came over and whispered, "I have to go pee pee." Mom is gonna hit the roof if I ask her if Dee can go to the bathroom, but before I could think of something, Dee knocked on the door and all hell broke loose. Mom screamed, "stop knocking on the damn door, little bitches!" I knew she'd get mad at us. She always called us bitches when she was really pissed off. So I took Dee to the sink, lifted her up, and she peed all over the sink and herself. We didn't have anything to wipe her with, so it went on her panties, too.

I ran to the bedroom to get her a change of clothes before mom came out of the bathroom. I changed Dee and got her back to the living room just in time. Mom came out of the bathroom with her clothes messed up and a big smile on her face. Our "uncle" who didn't seem to have a name this time, said, "Vienna, I gotta go, see you soon, ok."

Mom collapsed in the living room and fell asleep for a couple of hours.

A few weeks later, mom brought home a new "uncle" that we never saw before. This one had a name. His name was Brandon. He was huge! He stood 6' 8" and weighed a ton! Maybe like three hundred pounds! He had a deep voice and when he spoke, you knew he meant business! He was a well known drug dealer and always had bundles of cash on him. He'd give mom money for groceries and rent. So, mom was real happy. She'd always say that she didn't like him much, but the money was good.

Brandon hated that she went to bars and strip clubs. He'd always warn her that if he ever caught her in those places, he'd beat her ass. As usual, mom never listened. She headed out for the club one night and Brandon went looking for her. He was really mad. I was so scared for her. Oh Lord, if he finds mom, he's going to hit her. I can't tell Dee or else she'll cry. So, I waited to see what was going to happen. I heard later that when he caught up to her, he gave her a split lip and slapped her around.

When mom came back, she looked like she had been attacked by a dog. Brandon had put a real hurting on her this time! They would always get into physical fights, but this one was really a bad one! Mom's shirt was full of blood from her split lip. Her eye was swollen, and she was crying out of control. Mom had to go to the hospital for her busted lip. She had to get stitches. But, it seemed she never learned her lesson. One week after this incident, mom took Dee and me back to the strip club, sat us in the back of the club, behind the curtain, gave us chips and drinks, and then went up front in the club to dance topless with the other girls.

From time to time, I'd peak into the curtain and see mom dancing topless on men's laps and screaming, "whehewwww!!" Oh Lord, there she goes again. If Brandon finds out, he's going to beat her up again. Why doesn't she just listen? I don't want my mommy to get hurt again. But, if I go out there and try and stop her, then she's going to slap me! I'm tired of her slapping me. My face hurts! So, I sat there and played with Dee and colored in coloring books all night. Felt like we were there for days!

When I peeked in the curtain again, they were wilder! Mom and another girl were on top of one guy who was smiling and putting dollar bills in their panties. Guess Mom working at that diner wasn't bringing in enough money to support her drug habit. This is where she's getting the extra money for the drugs. And this is why we still have no furniture in our apartment. Mom keeps using all the extra money she earns for her drug habit. I hate drugs! I hate them! I hate them!

One night, while we were at the strip club, Brandon stormed in!! His face looked like a mean, mean devil. I got so scared, I grabbed Dee and ran into the bathroom. Brandon punched mom in the face and then kept slapping her around. The manager came over and tried to help her and he got hit, too!! Brandon dragged mom out of the club by her hair!!! She was freakin' out and said to him, "Brandon, get the hell off of me. I'm so sick of you!!" He pulled her harder and threw her into the car. Then, he went back inside and found us hiding in the bathroom and grabbed each of us with both arms and left the club. I thought he was going to hit us, but he didn't. He just kept yelling at mom all the way home.

It took mom a few days to forgive him, but she couldn't leave him, because the money was too good. So, when Brandon offered to let her live with him and his mom, she jumped at the chance. He had a lot of money and his mom was a great cook. She knew if we lived with him, all the pressure would be off of her. So, she accepted and we moved a week later. He had a nice apartment in Baltimore County. He had nice cars and he was very popular and extremely feared in the neighborhood.

Dee and I were really happy. We had settled in. Brandon's mom decided to make a chocolate cake one day and Dee and I decided to sample the cake. So, I took my little finger and ran my finger across the cake and then licked my finger. It was sooooo gooood! I told Dee to try it. She did and then we just kept doing it until we got caught by our mom. Mom yelled, "what the hell are you little bitches doin'?!!" She swore for about two minutes. Then she grabbed a piece of the cake and smashed it in my face! I was so shocked and started to cry. She did it over and over and then she did it to Dee. That got me really mad, because she was just a baby. I kept repeating over and over in my mind, "I hate you, I hate you!!"

By the time she was finished being mad at us, we had chocolate cake everywhere. It was in our hair, all over our clothes, and on the floor. Then mom screamed, "get the hell upstairs so I can wash you little bitches! You're always screwing things up for me! I can't stand you already!" So, we went upstairs with tears in our eyes and got cleaned up. I couldn't even look at her. I just wanted her to die right there, 'cause I was so mad at her! What did we ever do to her? She never liked us. Why? Why didn't she ever like us? Why? Oh, Lord, why? Then I began to cry more and she slapped me and told me, "stop acting like a baby!"

Vienna had threatened the girls not to say anything to Brandon. She did not want to upset him and besides he hated whenever she cursed at the girls. Lala and Dee complied, but acted out their anger in other ways. They would role play with their dolls and act out scenarios of what they really wanted to say to Vienna, but couldn't. Lala would always hit her doll and tell her, "I HATE YOU!" and Dee would always play hide and seek with her dolls, because she was always afraid.

More than a year passed and things were moving along well, when the family was hit with the worse news. Brandon was dead! He got caught up in a drug deal gone bad and was murdered. Vienna was devastated.

Another man of hers bites the dust. First Gary is sent to prison for life and now Brandon gets killed. She was convinced that her life was doomed. Here were these two little girls of hers and now no man to take care of them again. She knew that Brandon's mom would not let us stay.

She only did that for her son. With him gone, Brandon's mom asked Vienna and the girls to leave.

Vienna had no choice but to take them back to the projects. So, she packed them up and moved out. Lala was reenrolled into her old elementary school. Everything reverted back to the way things were before Vienna met Brandon. Vienna fell into a deep depression and started using drugs much more than ever before. She just couldn't handle the girls, the disappointments, and life in general.

Lala continued to take care of Dee as if she were her mother. She was left no choice, because Vienna was never around anymore. The girls were being neglected more and more. To make up for her absence, Vienna would make sure the girls had a good Christmas every year. She'd write down what each of them wanted and made sure they got everything on their lists. Easy bake ovens, Baby alive, and plastic Cinderella slippers, just to name a few.

"Oh Lord Dee, mom and her friends are locked in the bathroom again," Lala said. Lala knew this time it was a bad one. She could hear more people in the bathroom this time. They were talking loud and not making any sense. So, Lala got scared and banged on the door. Lala said, "hello, mom are you ok?" No one answered for a minute and then her mom flew open the door and looked down at Lala. Lala noticed her eyes were red and she looked like a monster. Vienna screamed, "Lala, get away from here now!" She slapped Lala so hard that everyone stopped and looked at Lala. Lala turned away in shame and ran to her room. She mumbled and mumbled, "I really hate her!"

Lala thought, "why does she keep slapping me? I'm not forgiving her this time and I'm going to stay mad." But, Lala never could. She would always forgive her mom, because she loved her. She knew those drugs were no good for her mom. So, she blamed the drugs and not her. She knew having her mother was better than not having her. Lala would ask God to take the drugs away from her mom, because they were hurting her more than helping her. But, mom wouldn't listen to God. She kept on doing the drugs.

One winter night, around eight, after being in our room all day, Dee and I were restless and hungry. We were alone in the apartment again. So, I decided to dress Dee and comb her hair. We set out to find our mother. I also knocked on a neighbors' door to see if they had any sandwiches. Dee began to cry from the hunger pains. I tried to comfort her, but I began to cry, too.

It was so scary to be in this big city and mom was not around. I felt like Dee's mother. I gave her baths, dressed her, fed her, played with her, and read books to her. I was only seven now and she was five, but we had each other. Mom knew I was mature for my age and kept leaving Dee with me. I was missing days of school just to take care of her. If I woke up in the morning and mom was not there, I knew I couldn't go to school.

Finally, one of our neighbors, Mrs. Green, opened her door. She looked down and saw Dee and I standing there. She said, "what in the world? Where is your mother?" We had to tell her the truth and expressed we were out looking for her. Mrs. Green let us in and told us to remove our coats. She served us pork chops, spaghetti, and red kool-aid. It was the best meal we ever had!!!

After we were done eating, Mrs. Green said, "I'm going to call the police on your mother." Dee started crying right away, because she didn't want mom to get in trouble. So, I had to think fast. I jumped up and said, "mom told us she was going to the store that was a little far away and would be back soon." Mrs. Green stared at me like she knew I was lying and told us to put our coats on. She instructed us to go straight back upstairs, seven floors up, and get back into our apartment.

I was so relieved that she didn't call the police right there. I grabbed Dee's hand and I hurried out her door. We were so scared that we ran up those seven flights of stairs like someone was chasing us!! When we got to the front of our apartment, we noticed the door had closed. We forgot that the door closes and locks automatically. We tried and tried, but couldn't get in. Dee kept saying she was cold. So, I remembered watching the Christmas show story of Bambi. Bambi and her mother were stuck in an ice storm in the middle of winter.

Bambi's mother had dug a hole for Bambi covered her with her body to keep Bambi warm. The next morning, Bambi's mother was dead. She had frozen to death, but Bambi survived. So, I decided to do the same thing. I made Dee lay down on the floor in front of the apartment door and then I laid down on top of her to keep her warm. I hugged her close so she wouldn't feel cold anymore.

I remember thinking that I could freeze to death like Bambi's mother. So, I told Dee how much I loved her. I'll never forget the way she turned and looked at me and said, "I love you, too." Then, she fell asleep. I could not fall asleep, because I was so afraid that I would die. So, I recited the Lord's prayer over and over. "Now I lay me down to sleep, I pray the Lord my soul to keep. If I should die before I wake, I pray the Lord my soul to take."

Praying was one of the best things that mom ever taught us. It always made me feel safe. Eventually, I must have fallen asleep, because mother woke us. When I opened my eyes, it was daylight. I was happy to be alive. I didn't die like Bambi's mom. Then mom screamed, "what the hell are you both doing out of the house?!" I saw a strange man standing next to her. One I had never seen before. When I tried to explain what happened, she just yelled more and told us to go to our room.

The same afternoon, the police showed up with Child Protective Services. I guess Mrs. Green didn't believe me and called to complain that we were being neglected by our mom. Mom insisted it was a lie and she had been there the whole time. So, they gave her a warning and told her that if they get another complaint that they would take us away from her. Dee started crying and saying she didn't want to leave mom. I took her to our room and started coloring books with her to keep her calm.

Later that day, Aunt Sharon came by to check us. Since we didn't have a phone, she would just pop up with food and things she thought we might need. Aunt Sharon got stern with mom and said, "Vienna, you are going to lose these kids if you don't straighten up fast!" Mom said nothing. She had this blank look on her face, as she often did. Aunt Sharon said, "ok, be that way!" She grabbed Dee and me and told us to come with her. Mom freaked out and ran into the kitchen and grabbed a butcher's knife!! She came charging out of the kitchen after Aunt Sharon. Aunt Sharon, shocked and angry, reached down and grabbed the big wheel on the floor and lunged it at her. Mom dropped the knife and fell to her knees.

Mom started to cry as she screamed out, "I want to die! I want my father!!" Aunt Sharon decided it was time to take charge and take mom to Spring Groves Mental Hospital. Mom's stay at the mental hospital was very short. She checked herself out three days later against medical advice. She picked up Dee and me from Aunt Sharon's house and went back home.

Aunt Sharon decided to help get mom a job at the Esskay Meat

Factory as a Security Officer. Mom got the job and things seemed like they were finally going to be okay. Dee and I never had a babysitter. I was always left with Dee instead. Mom couldn't afford babysitters. Sometimes, our relatives watched us if mom was going to be gone a long time or overnight.

One day, while mom was at work, I was feeding bread crumbs to the birds on the window ledge. Dee was in the kitchen playing with the stove. I was supposed to be watching her. Then, I smelled smoke. I said, "Oh Lord, Dee!" I ran into the kitchen to see what was happening and there were flames everywhere!!! I panicked and took Dee out of the kitchen. We were about to run out the front door, when Mom showed up with yet another "uncle." They grabbed pots of water and ran over to put out the flames.

After Mom and our new "uncle" put out the fire, mom started yelling at us and calling us dumb little bitches. She yelled, "Lala, you were supposed to be watching her!" She then turned her focus on Dee and said, "come here, since you like playing with fire, Take this!" She proceeded to grab Dee's little hand and burn her with a cigarette lighter. Dee started bawling and said, "I'm sorry." Mom ignored her apology and screamed out, "Now, how you like playing with fire, you little yellow ass bitch?!"

I was freaking out and then she turned the lighter on me and burned my hands with it. I confessed that I was not watching Dee, because I was trying to feed the birds on the window ledge. I decided to take the blame for everything, because Dee wasn't as strong as me. I didn't want her to get burned anymore. I took Dee into our room and hugged her really tight so she wouldn't be afraid. I refused to let her see me cry. I didn't want to worry her anymore than she already was, but when she fell asleep, I cried.

I wondered why mom treated us so mean. Why she didn't love us, even though we loved her. I used to watch The Jeffersons and Good Times and wonder why the parents never spoke to the kids the way mom spoke to us. I just thought, maybe we were really bad children. I felt so guilty that I would offer to help mom with just about everything. Mom had went into her room with our new "uncle" and when she came out, her whole face had changed. Yet, it didn't stop her from coming into our room and forcing us to promise not to tell anyone about the fire. She said that if we did, she would beat the hell out of us. So, we didn't tell anyone at all.

A couple of weeks later, while trying to get money for drugs, mom was arrested for shoplifting and sent to Jessup Correctional Facility for Women. Dee and I were home by ourselves when it happened. So, mom called Aunt Sharon to come and pick us up. Aunt Sharon told her that we could not stay with her for long. So, mom called Aunt Nilsa to pick us up from there. Since this was mom's third arrest, the judge sentenced mom to a year in prison.

I did not want Dee and I to go to Aunt Nilsa's house, because a few years earlier, her boyfriend had shot her in the stomach five times!! He had also shot her two daughters!! I was very scared of him. Now, both my mom and dad were in jail. I felt so alone. How was I going to take care of Dee by myself? Aunt Sharon knew how I was feeling and decided to start taking Dee and I for jail visits to mom and dad. They were actually across the street from each other. We would go see dad and then mom.

Every time mom saw us, she would cry and promise to be a better mom. She also kept promising to take us to the park and play with us. I really wanted to believe her. So, I'd tell Dee that she was telling the truth and she would be coming home soon. Meanwhile, we had to survive living with Aunt Nilsa and her violent boyfriend, Willy. That wasn't going to be easy. Aunt Nilsa's house was full. It was her, Willy, her two daughters, and now us. Recipe for disaster!!

Chapter Two
The Climb Out...

Aunt Nilsa was a mess! She was a very heavy drinker and smoker, as was her boyfriend, Willy. Against Willy's advice, Aunt Nilsa took us in. He was so angry about it that he sought out to make sure it wouldn't work. By now, I was eight and Dee was turning six. We attended our third school, Ashburton Elementary School, in Baltimore. Because we missed so much school from Vienna oversleeping and not taking us, we were made to repeat our last school year. I had to repeat the second grade and Dee had to repeat Kindergarten.

I will never forget my second grade school teacher, Ms. Wilkins. She showed a lot of concern for me. She would let me come over to her house sometimes after school and offer me extra help. She was extremely hard on me. So, when I asked her why, she said, "Because, I see great potential in you, Lala." That made me so happy. No one had ever said that to me before. So, I began to work harder. I started to do really well in school. But, home was a different story.

"Uncle" Willy was so mean. No matter how hard I tried, I could tell he didn't like me. He would give me more to do on purpose just to make me suffer. He would throw his dirty socks at me and they would hit my face. He'd laugh and walk off like he was a king or something. I couldn't stand him and his laugh was worse. He had this burly fake laugh. Every time I heard it, I just wanted to punch him in the face. One day, I was playing dolls with Dee, when he walked in and grabbed my doll out of my hand. I screamed, "hey, give me my doll back, Willy." He ran back over to me and pulled me by the hair and yelled, "you don't call me Willy, it's "Uncle" Willy to you, Lala!" I was so mad that I felt like slapping him in the face. So, I began to cry. That's what I would do whenever I got too mad to speak. He made me sick. I wished over and over that he'd get hit by a truck or something!!!

By the time I reached sixth grade, I had a teacher by the name of Ms. Turner. Ms Turner was my Math and Music teacher. She was the nicest lady you could imagine. I remember being in the spelling bee when I got my period for the first time. I felt this wet stuff coming down and I panicked. I thought I had peed on myself! I ran off stage and Ms. Turner ran right behind me. She asked, "Lala, where are you going and what's wrong?!" I was crying and confused. She stopped me from running and said, "Lala, this is natural. Girls get their "period" around this age." I looked at her and asked, "what is a period?" She laughed and replied, "ok, don't get scared, but look down. See this blood, it's called a period." I was afraid to look down, but when I did, I saw all this blood all over my panties and my pants. I panicked and slumped down in a stage chair. Ms. Turner hugged me tight and I was scared. So, I hugged her tighter.

Ms. Turner took me to the bathroom to get cleaned up and brought me a pair of pants from the lost and found box. They were too big, but I had to wear them until I got home. It felt funny walking with that pad between my legs all day long. It felt like everyone knew it was there. I didn't want anyone to make fun of me, so I never told anyone, not even Dee.

That year, I was scheduled to graduate from grade school. Ms. Turner was also my Home Room teacher. She taught me how to play the Clarinet. She also told me, "Lala, you really have a beautiful voice and I want you to sing at the graduation." I blushed and told her, "I'd do anything she asked me to." I loved her and she had replaced my other teacher, Ms. Wilkins, in my life. Ms. Wilkins had retired by the time I reached the sixth grade.

The song that Ms. Turner chose for me to sing was one of my favorites called "Over the Rainbow." A song I could sing really well. I also received a $100.00 savings bond for most improved student! I'll never forget when my named was called for the bond. I felt like a winner at the Grammy's! Everyone was cheering, including my mother, Vienna, who showed up by surprise with Aunt Nilsa. Aunt Nilsa had bought me a yellow and white graduation dress with white shoes. As I stood up on stage, I got "cold feet." Ms. Turner had played the introduction to the song, but I froze. Nothing came out of my mouth. She then played it again and whispered,

"I believe in you. You can do it." Just then, the words began to flow out of my mouth and I began to sing as if I were Patti LaBelle or something!! I could hear my mother yelling through the crowd, "that's my baby!"

Oh Lord, Mama is gonna make a fool of herself. I knew she was proud of me, but I didn't want her to yell out loud! After the graduation ceremony, everyone came up to me to congratulate me. I immediately received two acceptance letters from two vocational/technical school programs for a full scholarship! The catch was I had to have a way to and from the school. Aunt Nilsa didn't drive, so I had to go to Pimlico Middle School. I had to catch the public MTA bus to go to school. By now, I was twelve. The school I really prayed for was the Baltimore School of Arts. I had always dreamed of being an actress. I was not accepted to that school, because we could not afford the tuition. I cried and cried until my tears dried out.

I later found out that "Uncle" Willy had a wife with three children across town. Yet, he decided to stay with Aunt Nilsa instead. Willy hated Aunt Nilsa's eldest daughter, Nina the most. I don't know why. He just did. Nina would try to reach out to her real Dad, who lived with his new wife and their two children, to help her with dealing with Willy. I don't think Willy had a good side. He rubbed all of us the wrong way. I never could understand why Aunt Nilsa dealt with such a monster. Everything I did seemed to bother him, no matter how hard I tried. If I didn't clean something right, he'd call me everything but the child of God. I always caught the heat, even if it was Dee who did something wrong.

Why did Aunt Nilsa stay with a man who tried his best to kill her? Didn't she love herself? Was she confused or something? Maybe she should go and talk to God like I do.

God can help you with anything if you just confide in Him. I just know He can.

I would try to stay out of Willy's way as much as possible. After awhile, I'd get creative with it. I'd ask Aunt Nilsa to let me go to a friend's house on the weekend just to get away from him. I loved to Roller Skate. So, every Saturday I'd go to the famous Rhythm Skate on the west side of Baltimore near Liberty Heights. Everybody who was anybody would show up there. It became so popular that we formed skate groups. Our group was called the TSS, which meant "The Sexy Seven." We wore red hoodies with our names on the back. You couldn't tell us nothing! We were as bad as we wanted to be!!

Rhythm Skate was so popular that rappers like LL Cool J, Heavy D, The Fat Boys, Roxanne Shante, and New Edition to name a few. They were incredibly cool. They'd take pictures with us, sign autographs, and were just blending in like regular folks. Not like it is now. "Hollywood Types" don't usually mingle today like they did yesterday.

One day, when I was sitting outside on the steps with my best friends, Roxy and Jayla, I told them about everything I was going through. I made them promise not to repeat anything I had said. While I was outside talking to them, Willy walked passed us in a huff like he was mad at the world. Aunt Nilsa was inside making lunch for all of us, when we heard her scream. I ran inside to see what was going on. Willy had Aunt Nilsa by the throat and screaming, "I hate you. You ruined my life!"

Aunt Nilsa was turning white and trying to get his hands away from her neck, but he wouldn't let go. I ran in and told them that everyone outside could hear what was going on. He ignored me like I wasn't even there. So, I jumped on him and started scratching and biting him. He let Aunt Nilsa go and focused on me. He grabbed me by the throat and lifted me off the floor like a rag doll. I thought I was dying. His grip was so strong I couldn't even scream! He looked into my eyes with such a hatred and said, "you little yellow bitch, you should have minded your business, I'm going to kill you!" I got so scared that I started praying, "please God, if he kills me, take care of Dee and Mommy for me." My face felt so tight that I thought I was going to burst! Aunt Nilsa started breathing better and finally ran over to us and pleaded with him to let me go. He dropped me to the floor and I started gasping and struggling for air.

Since I was thirteen now, he was getting more and more aggressive. He thought he owned us and could do whatever he wanted. I hated him with a passion and he knew it. So, he kept paying me back for that every chance he got! That bastard made me sick. I vow to get him back one day. I didn't know yet what I was going to do, but I knew I had to do something to make him go away! On Saturday nights, Aunt Nilsa loved to go out dancing and once she got started, even wild horses couldn't stop her hips from moving! That night, when Aunt Nilsa got home, Dee and I were already sleeping. That's when all hell broke loose! Willy was drunk and acting a fool. He lunged up and I knew this was going to be a really bad night!

Willy began to really lay into Aunt Nilsa! This time it was different. It was more violent than ever before. He hit her so many times that I thought he was in a boxing ring fighting a man!!! She was screaming like he was killing her! I wanted to help her, but after what he did to me, I was petrified. So, I did nothing this time. After he got all his aggravation out on her, he left the house. Aunt Nilsa yelled out, "I hate you and that bitch you cheating on me with. Go, go back to her. I know that's what you want!!"

I sneaked into the room and saw Aunt Nilsa laying on the bed. She was crying a lot. She had a black eye and she was bleeding from her nose. I could feel her sadness. Her heart was broken. I never wanted to feel like that. Why are men so mean?! Why do good women always have to suffer?! She didn't deserve this. He's such a jerk!! She needs to get rid of him. Should I tell her that? Will she even listen to me?

I went over to her and told her not to worry. I told her that God was with her. I told her to pray and that everything will be ok. I went and got a warm wash cloth and cleaned the blood off her face. I thanked her for taking care of us and now I was going to take care of her. I helped her get undressed and put her nightgown on. I laid her back down on the bed and she felt so weak. Like the wind had been knocked out of her heart.

Aunt Nilsa was also drunk, too. So, she couldn't let it go. She kept cursing and crying at the same time.

She was calling Willy names and repeating over and over, "I hate you, Willy. I hate you!!" Little did we know that Willy had come back into the house! He ran back into the bedroom and zoned in on me. He grabbed me by the shirt and screamed, "what you been saying little bitch? Why you keep getting in my damn business? I had enough of you!!" He balled up his fist and punched me dead in the face. I fell into the dresser and blacked out. Our relatives that were upstairs heard everything.

Aunt Marie and some other relatives came running downstairs and stopped Willy from going crazy. I was carried upstairs and they put cold water on my face. I awoke and started crying, because my face hurt so bad. He hit me again!! I can't believe that monster. The boogie man does exist. His name is Willy!! I was put in my cousin, Doc's room, to sleep for the night. I was so depressed. I just couldn't take it anymore. I was mad at Willy, I was mad at my Mom, and I was mad at God. There was so much I didn't understand. I want to be a kid, but I could never be one. Not ever!!

The next morning, I packed a bag, and took Dee and we ran away. I had had enough of everyone. I felt like no one was on my side. I went from house to house of each one of my friends. The parents were suspicious. They kept asking me a lot of questions. I finally ran out of lies and one of them brought me back to Aunt Nilsa's. By this time, our Mom, Vienna, was out of jail and living with her new boyfriend. She never came back for me or Dee. I called her and begged her to bring us home, but she said, "no, Lala. My new boyfriend, Gerry, doesn't have the patience for kids." What?! She chose him over us! What kind of mother is that?!!!!

I had no choice but to stick it out at Aunt Nilsa's. I did everything I could to avoid Willy. He had the worse liquor breath ever! His mouth smelled like the booze was on fire or something! I wanted to throw up every time he screamed in my face. So, I'd get up real early and head out to school before time. When school was over, I'd go to my friend's houses and stay late. When I came back home, I'd go to my room and try not to see him. I was tired of being hit and yelled at. So, I did not want to give him any reason, any reason at all to come at me, yell at me, or hit me.

During this time, a kid named Taye kept trying to get me to go out with him. He was cute, light skinned, and sweet. But, I didn't like him like that. He seemed more like a brotherly type than anything else. I was more interested in his best friend, Mark. Who was tall, dark, and handsome. I didn't want to tell Taye about it, because I didn't want to hurt his feelings. So, I said nothing. Taye walked me home one day. He looked at me and said, "ok, run, I will give you a head start. If I catch you, you have to agree to go out with me and kiss me, too." I thought I could outrun him, so I agreed. I took off running and he kept gaining on me. I was so surprised he could run that fast. Oh Lord, he's going to win!!

He yelled out, "here I come!!" He caught up to me and wrestled me to the ground. He started tickling me. He was so excited and screamed out, "I got you!" I paused and looked at him and then he kissed me. We agreed not to tell anyone just yet. I backed myself into a corner and now I have to go out with him. Great! Just great!!

It was an exhausting school year, but I made it!! I was so looking forward to the summer. I couldn't wait to hang out with my friends! One summer day, while I was at a friend's house, Taye, Mark, and a few of my girlfriends came by to hang out.

Little did I know that that day would alter our lives forever. Like boys often do, they like to horse around and push the boundaries of competition. Taye and Mark were challenging each other to Russian roulette. They took a gun, put one bullet in it, and took turns pulling the trigger. Nuts!!! Oh, Lord, it was such a dangerous game. How come boys are so daring?! Well, we were outside and had no idea what they were doing.

Next thing I know a loud pop rang out!! It sounded like a thunder bolt or something! We ran inside to see what happened and Taye was lying on the floor. This time, the bullet didn't miss. He had shot himself in the head. I was in absolute shock.

Last week he had told me he wanted to go into the army like his older brother. I had told him that I wanted to be a nurse. We had just completed the seventh grade! How could this have happened?!!

I was in disbelief. I didn't want to believe it was real. But, when I looked down, Taye's blood and brains were all over the floor and wall!! Right in front of my face and in broad daylight. I fainted. The following week, I was attending his funeral.

This was the same guy that had chased me for a block to kiss me. I stood there even more shocked. I was wearing the same yellow and white dress that I used for graduation a year earlier. I could see the bullet hole in his face and a patch of hair had been added to the top of his head to cover where the bullet had exited. Dear God, this just don't make no sense. Why God? Why? I really took Taye's death pretty hard. To this day, I still can't sleep without a light being on. It was a hard summer to get through.

Taye's death made me so depressed. It felt like life was so unfair and my innocence was destroyed even more. He was so young. He played with fire and he lost. It made me afraid to go outside or visit anyone. I tried to keep my mind busy, but the vision of him lying on the floor kept coming back to me over and over. Like a movie that wouldn't stop. I was unable to erase the memory and I wondered how do I get pass this and not go crazy? It also reminded me of another kid named Preston, who was in the eighth grade, and met the same fate. He played the roulette game and loss, too.

I decided to flood my mind with things to do and block it out as much as I can. Summer was over and my eighth grade school year began. I signed up for The West Side Marching Band as a majorette. I also went roller skating every weekend. The rest of my free time went to babysitting. I was determined not to be around Willy or think about Taye. Incidently, it made me happy that I agreed to go out with Taye and let him kiss me. I now realized that I was the only girlfriend he would ever have. That gave me peace that I had not rejected him even though I wanted to.

Aunt Nilsa had stipulated me to an eleven o'clock curfew. One Friday night, since I didn't want to be late, I made sure not to miss the bus. I got off on my block and started walking toward the house. From where I was, I could actually see Aunt Nilsa sitting on the porch drinking and singing away. An uneasy feeling came over me and it made me turn around.

A man was walking close behind me. I started walking faster and so did he! My heart started racing as he got closer. He said, "how are you doing?" Confused, I replied, "Hello, I'm fine." He stated that was good and kept walking next to me. Then, made his move. He grabbed me, put one of his hands over my mouth, and held a knife to my throat. Oh my God, I was so damn scared! My life started to flash before my eyes. What do I do? What do I do?

I decided to fight! As I started to bite him and scratch him, he let me go for a split second. I thought I was free, but he grabbed me by the throat and pushed me up against a neighbors van that was parked right near Aunt Nilsa's house. He whispered in my ear, "I am going to kill you." I pretended to see my cousin Dante and kept screaming out to him as if he were there. The man punched me in the face and I got so mad that I kicked the knife out of his hand. When he bent down to pick up the knife, I took off running and screaming for holy hell!!

The man, who was wearing red sweatpants and a yellow shirt, ran. He thought Dante was coming over to help me. I reached Aunt Nilsa's duplex house, where she was still singing. She could tell I was in a panic. She brought me inside and called the police. My cousin, Dante, realizing what was going on, took off running with some friends to find the guy.

My face was so swollen from the punch he gave me to the face. Blood was overflowing in my mouth. I thought he broke my teeth, but he didn't. He had only cut my lip open. I could barely sleep that night. Every time I dozed off, I saw his face and I jumped up screaming. I really thought he was going to kill me right there! I was shaking and crying. It freaked me the hell out! Damn bastard, why didn't I scratch his eyes out?!!!

The next morning, not more than two miles away from where the man had attacked me, a fourteen year old black girl was found raped and murdered!! He left her behind a church on Park Heights Avenue. That could have been me!! Oh, Lord, that could have been me!!! Thank God for the courage he gave me to be brave enough to fight that monster off!! My sassiness came in handy and saved my life!!

At that time, we lived in the west side of Baltimore, a mostly working class neighborhood that was much better than the east side housing projects we came from. Although I had never felt safe at Aunt Nilsa's house, I loved her and was incredibly grateful to her for taking Dee and I in, even though Willy didn't want us there. She had a duplex house that allowed her to have her family occupy the upstairs.

Her two sisters, Aunt Marie and Aunt Betsy lived there. Aunt Marie lived there with her boyfriend Jim and son Dean. Aunt Betsy had no children or husband. She just concentrated on helping her sisters raise their kids instead. I was very close to my cousin Dean. He and I were only one year apart. Aunt Marie was the best cook in the world! I would sleep up there most nights just to stay out of Willy's way, because I was still so afraid of him.

One night, while I was sleeping upstairs in Dean's room, I opened my eyes and saw Jim standing over me. He was fondling my breasts and signaling with his other hand for me to stay quiet. I froze. I was so mad at him, but I was afraid he'd beat me like Willy did before, so I let him touch me. I only told Jayla, my best friend, what Jim had done. She couldn't believe it. She really felt sorry for me. I also didn't want to tell Aunt Marie, because I didn't want to break her heart.

From that day on, I kept an eye on Jim. Whenever no one was looking, he'd grab a feel of my breasts and then give me five dollars so I wouldn't tell anyone. That made me feel even worse. Like he thought I was a whore or something. I found myself crying a lot and being very rebellious.

I was very well built for my age. I was five feet tall, but my bra size had already reached a 36DD. So, I received a lot of attention from many guys at school. Even older men whistled and gawked at me while I was walking to and from school. The kids actually nicknamed me "Boom Boom Belinda."

I rarely had a problem with getting boyfriends or having so-called crushes
come my way. Aunt Nilsa dubbed me the worse fourteen year old kid in the world, because I was acting out, talking grown, and being fresh in school.

I couldn't confide in anyone, but my closest friends about what I was going through. I also didn't want to be away from Dee. I felt like a hampster trapped in a cage. I was so unhappy. I felt so alone. Whenever I went upstairs, I got molested by Uncle Jim. There were horrible moments, like him pulling out his penis and making me touch it, while he fondled my breasts.

Back downstairs, Uncle Willy would curse and beat me up all the time. Even though things were really bad, I'd think about the girl who was raped and killed instead of me. I'd think of Taye and feel sad that he shot himself dead. It had been a year and I still wasn't over it. I got knots in my stomach when I went back to it in my memory. I just couldn't erase the image I had of him lying on the ground. It frightened me to no end.

At one point Uncle Jim got bold enough to call me to his room at night to watch porno movies. I'd say no, but he'd drag me onto the bed and force me to watch. He'd say in a very low voice, "That's what I want to do to you and I will soon." I'd start shaking and think that I couldn't possibly be capable of doing those nasty things. My mind just had not advanced that far.

Since I could not confide in anyone in the house, I fell into a really deep depression. I was afraid of adults. They were so mean and violent to me that I became a recluse while at home. Then one day, my best friend Jayla brought me to her mother Eve's house. She was from Jamaica. She was very authoritative and stern with me. She said in a motherly voice, "Lala, I need you to be straight with me and tell me what you are going through right now." At first, I hesitated and began to cry. She was patient and told me, "Lala, we are not moving from this spot until you tell me the whole truth. I got all day."

She cornered me, so I had no choice. I started to tell her everything. It all came out and I felt so relieved, because I had been carrying it around all by myself. The load and the pain was overwhelming. I didn't realize how bad it had gotten until I shared it with her. She made me feel safe. After all, I waited for her response. She said nothing for about a minute or two and then she replied, "I believe you, Lala. I really do." I had been holding my breath and breathed a sigh of relief when I saw that she believed me. Finally, someone believed me!!

The more I cried, the more Juju's mom, Eve, eyes swelled up with tears. I explained to her, "Ms. Eve, I don't know what to do, because, Dee and I have no other place to go. So, I asked her to promise me that she wouldn't do anything to get Aunt Nilsa into trouble. Ms. Eve said, "Ok, I promise, but I want you over here as much as possible, ok?!" I agreed and became a fixture at her home as often as I could.

She included me in everything at her home. She made me part of her family and I came to consider her as my Godmother. She gave me chores to do around the house, like weeding and gardening. She even included me as an Usher in her son's wedding. I wore a traditional Jamaican dress, called a Sari. I started spending nights over, even school nights, too.

Ms. Eve's husband, James, was a Firefighter. He was actually drinking buddies with Willy! James told Willy what was going on and Willy tried to stop me from staying over there at night. Ms. Eve knew what they were up to and did her best to sneak me in at night whenever James had to sleep over at the Fire House. On his days off, she would sneak us into one of the owner's houses she cleaned and let us spend the night there when they weren't home.

Ms. Eve did her best to protect me. I saw her as my fairy Godmother. She was a very good housekeeper and never had a problem with her clients. So, they were willing to do anything for her, because she was so nice. Later on, I realized that James, who was 350lbs and 6 feet tall, was abusing Ms. Eve, who was only 115lbs and five feet tall. That made me really mad!! I wanted to ball up my fists and punch him in the head!!! These men were stupid and mean and I didn't like them!!!

Aunt Nilsa had two girls who were older than Dee and I. The youngest one had gone off to college and the oldest one, who had suffered the same fate of sexual abuse I did, moved out and had a baby. She had turned to drugs to cope with the dysfunction and pain she endured living with her mom. She also stayed as far away from the house as she could.

I was very angry as a child, so I would often get into a lot of trouble in school. I would pick fights in school in order to get in trouble and hopefully cause them to put me in a foster home. I figured Dee would be alright, because she was two years younger and everyone treated her like the baby. So, I was shocked to learn that Aunt Marie's boyfriend was sexually abusing Dee! I flipped out!!! I told my neighbor and also wrote a letter to my father in jail telling him everything.

After receiving my letter in prison, my Dad called the house immediately to speak to Aunt Nilsa. He shouted, "Sis, what the hell is going on over there?!! Aunt Nilsa, who didn't know what was happening, didn't know how to respond. She looked shocked, but managed to say, "This is the first time I'm hearing about this crap. I don't know what's going on!" Right after the call, she accused me of being a trouble making bitch.

She also banned me from ever going upstairs again. She treated me as if I was ungrateful and unthankful. But, that wasn't true. I just wanted the abuse to stop. I didn't even care anymore if Aunt Nilsa is mad at me. By this point, I realized that she could no longer protect Dee and me. In my mind, she had failed to keep us safe from the monsters living in her house and I was really sick of it all. I wanted out.

Dee chose to block out everything, which was even worse than dealing with it. She acted as if nothing had happened. She never wanted to talk about it or defend us. Since my dad and I were very close, we were writing to each other every week. In my very next letter, I wrote and begged him to get me the hell out of that house, which now had eleven people living in it! It became a Zoo. Aunt Marie's son, who had spent a few years in prison for robbing a bank, moved into the basement of the duplex with his girlfriend.

Dad came through for me! He made arrangements for me to move to Alberquerqee, New Mexico. His sister, Lorna, a divorced College Professor with one son, had a house there. It was rumored that she was a closet lesbian with a female lover named Jane living right next store to her. Oh Lord, made me feel like the grass was not greener on the other side! My family had always played tug of war with Dee and I. My head was spinning by this time.

Aunt Lorna was not an angel by far. She was a heavy marijuana smoker. She and Jane were smoking buddies and often invited me to smoke with them! I refused at first, but they kept pressing me until I joined in. They explained to me that it would take the edge off my stress and it would calm me down. Aunt Lorna was like, "look, you take on too much, this will help you stay relaxed."

Since she was the adult, I figured she knew what she was talking about. What harm could it do? So, I started joining them more often. Marijuana made me feel high. She never explained that part. Why was I feeling like I couldn't feel anything inside? I felt funny. I wasn't thinking straight. I couldn't concentrate, so I began cutting classes, which defeated the fact that I had finally gotten ahead and was in the right grade. I was glad to be in tenth grade and be with the right aged class.

I had turned fifteen and was attending Moriarty Senior High School. At first, I was doing really well and that's how I advanced to the right grade. But, after being invited to my Aunt Lorna's marijuana circus, I found myself going in the wrong direction. Aunt Lorna was more like a friend instead of an authoritative figure. She was suppose to love and protect me not let me smoke and get wild.

I could not go on like this. I was trying to fit in where I didn't belong. I was out of control and getting worse. So, the more I couldn't deal with life, the more I smoked. I was hooked on pot. What a disaster I had become. I wasn't thinking straight and I didn't even care at this point. I wondered how my mom and Dee were doing and I missed them.

Chapter Three
The Road Back Home…

Aunt Lorna and her lover Jane were always at each other's throats. Jane was mad, because Aunt Lorna was having second thoughts about being a lesbian and wanted to go back to dating men. Jane was furious, because she loved Lorna and didn't want to break up. I was being pulled in different directions. They would both come and vent their feelings to me like I was a psychologist or something.

Jane had had it one day and pulled me to the side and said, "I'm so tired of Lorna. She thinks she can just get rid of me like I'm a dog. She's playing with my feelings and I can't take her anymore." I just stood there with this blank look on my face like do you have a joint I can smoke, because I can't take Jane anymore. Then Aunt Lorna would grab me by the arm and take me into her house.

"What did Jane say to you, tell me everything," Aunt Lorna persisted. She was determined to use me as the go between. I finally had had enough. I told her, "Aunt Lorna, thanks for everything, but I miss home and I don't belong here." She was shocked at first and then she just slumped in her chair and realized that she turned me into a rebel that was lost.

One evening, while at Aunt Lorna's house, my mom called! I was so excited to here her voice that I almost fainted. "Lala, come home," she said softly. I had waited my whole life to hear those words!! She went on to explain that Dee missed me terribly, that she was sick, and that we needed to be a family again. I asked her about her boyfriend Gerry and she convinced me that he knew and agreed to take me back. Whew! This was my mother and I loved her still with everything I had in me.

She said Gerry had changed his mind about everything and would welcome me with open arms. I asked her, "Mom, are you still on drugs?" She said, "I'm in a drug treatment program." I later found out that she was attending a Methadone Clinic, which is basically a legal way to get a different drug. Mom chimed in, "Lala, we're going to have the life I always dreamed of." Mom would always say that we were going to live in the Village of Cross Keys, where Oprah lived. That was always her dream. Oprah had lived on the north west side of Baltimore in a gated apartment complex.

I agreed to return to Baltimore, but my excitement was shortlived. I found out shortly after I got there that Mom had tricked me into returning to her so she could apply for a welfare check and food stamps. The very next day that I arrived, she marched me right down to the Welfare office and filed for assistance. I confirmed that I now lived with her and she was approved for benefits.

What a low down dirty shame! Mom just wasn't done playing games! Luring me to Baltimore so that she could collect!! Come on, what else was going to go wrong. Dee was still living at Aunt Nilsa's and mom had not made arrangements for her to live with us like she had promised. I was so turned off that it made me sick.

I decided to get a job and attend school so that I could keep my mind off of this. Since I was only fifteen, I lied and said I was eighteen on the application to work at Burger King. It worked!! I knew it would, because I didn't look my age, I looked older. Besides, I wanted him to treat me like an adult and not a child. He did and also let me work as many hours as I wanted.

I started saving so much money. I'd get out of school at 2:30pm and go straight to work. I stayed busy and things were fine for several weeks. Gerry was barely seeing me and that's why he hadn't cursed or hit me and oddly I began to feel safe. Until the night all hell broke loose!!

At that time, Gerry wasn't using drugs, but he was still a heavy drinker. One night, when he got home late, he called to Mom, "Vienna where's my dinner?!" Mom was afraid to answer, but mustered, "Gerry, I prepared ground meat patties, but I didn't want to cook them until you came home so your dinner wouldn't be cold." She was trembling, because she could feel him begin to get enraged.

Gerry wasn't satisfied with her answer and flew off in a rage, "you lazy ass bitch!!" He threw the raw meat on the floor, grabbed my mom by the hair, and pushed her face down into the ground right into the raw meat!! He started to punch, kick, and shove her face into the meat over and over. He kept calling her a lazy bitch. He beat her so bad that her face was bloody.

Later, when he left, I begged mom to get our stuff and go into a shelter. She said, "No Lala, we have to stay here." She said it was all her fault that that had happened and that everything would be ok. She tried to convince me that Gerry was a good man and took real good care of us, but that he was just drunk.

Then she shocked me by saying, "Lala, maybe you should go until he cools off again." What?!! I wasn't even involved in their argument. I told her that I didn't have anywhere to go. She thought it would be for the best and didn't want to take a chance of him taking it out on me. She said sadly, "Lala, I think you should leave now before he comes back."

Oh Lord, it was 01:00am!! It was summertime. Where was I going to go?! I went and got dressed and walked out of the house. I started walking towards Baltimore's Inner Harbor, which was miles away. Where mom was living with Gerry was a small row house near downtown Baltimore. It felt like I had walked for miles and miles. I was looking at homeless people and praying that I didn't end up like them. I finally sat down on a bench and just cried.

Praying for God to help me, I said, "God, please, I've done all I can, can you take over now?" What else was I supposed to do? Then, Dawn came. I felt safer with the Sun up and started to walk back toward's Mom's house.

When I got home, thankfully, Gerry wasn't there. He had left for work already. Mom was up and strangely she didn't even ask me where I had gone. She whispered to me, "Lala, go get something to eat and go to your room." Her face had turned completely black and blue. I felt so sorry for her. Why didn't she want to leave? She must be really afraid of Gerry. I hate him. I wished he were dead so he couldn't hurt her anymore. That bastard.

Months went by and things only got worse. Gerry kept beating up Mom like she was a rag doll or something. He took all of his frustration out on her. Believe it or not, he was a short guy. He had spent four years in the army and learned a lot of fighting tactics. All of which I think he used against my mom. Mom's drug habit escalated from the physical and mental abuse he was handing her.

She went from doing drugs in the bathroom to cooking and doing drugs in my room! I couldn't say anything, because I didn't want her to throw me out. I will never forget the first time I saw her doing drugs. It made me feel sad for her. She had certain supplies for her drug kit. She would always have her matches, a bottle top, cotton from her cigarette, and water.

It was the worse smell. I can still smell it. She would then tie one of my socks around her arm, stick a needle in one of her veins with a syringe, and proceed to shoot up her drugs. It must have felt good, because she would always roll her eyes up as if it was. I would walk in and grab the syringe and see all her blood in it. It drove me crazy, so I would tell her, "Mom, why are you doing drugs and hurting yourself?!" She would always defend herself and respond, "Lala, I'm a grown ass woman and I'll do what the hell I want to do. Stop asking me so many damn questions and mind your damn business!"

She had the nerve to tell me that she used my room, because she knew Gerry never came in my room. It made it easy for her to hide her drugs and shoot up in private. She was out of control. This went on for many weeks. Then one day Gerry came home and told us, "my dad shot and killed himself." His dad had been dating a younger woman, who had decided to leave him and go back to her old boyfriend.

I guess he was so hurt that he didn't want to live anymore. So, he got real drunk that day and put the gun in his mouth and blew his brains out. Sad. Gerry became even colder and drifted into an even deeper depression.

The following day, Thursday December 05, 1985, I went to school and then work. When I came home, I checked to see if the money I had saved from working was still there. Eighty dollars was missing!! So, I asked my mom if she had took it. She replied, "yes, Lala, I took it. Gerry had given me money to pay the phone bill and I used it to get high. I needed it, because I was feeling sick." I didn't understand how getting high could make her sickness go away.

I was so pissed at her. I had worked all those hours to save that money and now she stole it from me. She continued, "Lala, I took your money to pay the bill. I'll pay you back." I was so damn upset, but I didn't want her to see that, because even though I was mad at her, I still loved her. After all, she was my mother.

I went to be alone. When I finally was, being mad about it, I cried saying to myself, "I hate her and I hope she dies!" I didn't really mean it, but I was just mad at her and I had to let it out. I asked her, "Mom, can I go over my friend's house for the weekend?" She surprisingly said, "yes. Go ahead, Lala." I was so relieved, because I didn't want to yell at her and I thought getting away from her for the weekend would let me cool off a bit.

That next day, Friday, after school, my friend Jenny and her mother came to pick me up. As I was leaving, Mom came to see me out and told me, "Lala, I love you." She hugged and kissed me. I said, "mom, don't worry, see you Sunday night, I'll be ok. I love you, too." I was very mad at her. She was still high when I left.

That Saturday, December 08, 1985, at 9:00pm, Gerry called, telling me that my mother had died!!! She was just thirty five. What the hell happened!! I was in a state of shock. I was told she had taken an overdose of drugs. I called my Dad, who was still in prison, and said in a soft voice, "Daddy, she's gone. Mom overdosed on a mixture of methadone and prescription pills." I couldn't even cry. I was in such disbelief. Although she wasn't the best mother in the world, she was still my mother and I loved her so much. Lately, we had become friends, despite her stealing from me. She was simply all I had.

We would talk about everything now that I was older. She confided in me about her past, my father, and her family. I did not know what I was going to do without her being here. It felt like such a huge void! A pain I never imagine I'd ever feel. Now, at fifteen, I was again homeless with absolutely nowhere to turn. I had all these thoughts of panic swirling in my head, but the one that kept repeating over and over was what now???

My friend Jenny's mom agreed to let me stay with them for a few weeks. Aunt Sharon came by to pick me up for the funeral services. She was always taking care of everything down to the details. She had picked out a beautiful white dress for mom with matching jewelry for the wake. I tried being involved as much as I could, but I was feeling incredibly guilty for wishing the week before that she had died for taking the eighty dollars from me. I couldn't shake the guilt. I felt so responsible for what happened to her. I kept blaming myself for that wish coming true.

If I had not saved that money, she wouldn't have been able to buy the drugs! I was so mad at her, but I didn't mean for her to die. It was just a figure of speech I had learned from the friends and family around me. They said it all the time when they got mad. So it just came out automatically in my mind. I was saving that money for us to move to a better place. I felt so violated, because she had stolen the money from me behind my back. That moment taught me that you'd better be careful of what you do and say, because you just might live to regret it.

Aunt Sharon tried her best to get me to go up to the coffin and view my mom's body, but I vehemently refused. I just couldn't do it! Two days before, my mom was alive and sporting a huge smile when I left. I sneaked a look from far away from where the coffin was and I didn't even recognize her. When she was alive, mom had this beautiful caramel complexion and curly black shiny hair. Now, she was so dark with too much makeup on her face that it made her look like an old lady.

Nonetheless, she was still beautiful. Her boyfriend, Gerry, was there. There was also another man there next to him that I didn't recognize. They were both drunk and crying. They kept taking turns going up to her casket and kissing her dead body while she laid in that coffin. I remember thinking she just looks like she's taking a nap. I wanted her to wake up any minute and say she was ok, but that never happened. My mom was gone and I really didn't know how to go on without her.

That stranger that was with Gerry went up to the casket one too many times and Gerry got furious at him. A fight broke out between them right there!! Gerry was so angry and was flaying fists at him screaming, "what the fuck are you doing, man?!!" The guy was in shock and started fighting back!

My grandmother got so upset and yelled out, "this is just ridiculous! Can't I bury my daughter in peace?! Look at these fools!!" So my Uncles all got in gear and broke up the fight and forced both of them to settle down. You could cut the tension with a knife! I was sitting in the lobby of the funeral home. Though I couldn't bring myself to go in near mom's coffin, I could hear everything. Someone read a poem that compared my mother to a fading flower that water could not save. That made me so sad. Recently, mom had been a beautiful flower, like a pink rose.

It was almost like she was two people. When she wasn't high, she was so much fun. I remember we would watch T.V. together and laugh. I can still see her laying in bed with her Pepsi can, snickers, and cigarettes, which her favorite three things to have.

As I was thinking of our memories, my Uncle Allen came out to persude me to go in. The funeral was coming to an end and everyone was talking about getting me in there. I hesitated at first, but finally decided to go in. I kept silently praying with every hard step I took.

All I could think was, oh Lord, don't let me faint in there!! Uncle Allen said, "Lala, you have to go in and say goodbye. This will be the last time you ever get to see your mother again." I was starting to cry and grabbed Uncle Allen's hand. He walked me up slowly. When I reached her coffin, I lost it!! All I could muster was, "why God, why?!!!" Privately, I thought, I didn't really mean what I said. Why God, why did you take my mom from me? It broke my heart. I could not believe my eyes and everyone started getting nervous around me. I heard whispers, "maybe we shouldn't have brought her up there. Someone needs to get her out. This is too much for her!"

When I wiped my tears away, I imagined it was me instead of her in the coffin. We looked so much alike, but I was much lighter, because I took after my dad. I went back to my conversation with God and just kept asking, "why God, why?" I tried to explain to God that I didn't mean what I said and that I didn't really want her to drop dead like this. Please God, I take it back. I take it back! I was only upset about the money, God. I only wanted us to go to a better life. Bring her back, God. Please, bring her back. God, I'll do anything you ask, just bring her back to me.

It was all too much and ultimately I collapsed to the floor in tears. People rushed up and picked me up and guided me out. It got chaotic to say the least. People started blaming each other for me being allowed in. There were like ten arguments going on at once and I had to get out of there just to breathe.

Then, the reality set in. I had no father to live with, because my dad was still in jail. I had nowhere to turn to and nowhere to go. Going back to Aunt Nilsa's was out of the question. I'd rather be on the street then ever go back to that Zoo. What now, God? What now? It was finally time that I truly needed to take a walk with God. I had no idea which way to turn.

My Uncle Ronnie, who loved my mother more than life, blamed himself for mom's death. He solemnly said, "it's all my fault. I was the one who introduced to heroin." He felt that if it wasn't for him, she would have never even tried drugs. Uncle Ronnie fell into a very deep depression and started to drink and do drugs more than ever.

I remember when he took Dee and I to see his kids, Rob and Danny, along with his girlfriend Trina. He lived with Trina at the time. They had a volatile relationship. Uncle Ronnie had a very short fuse. Every time he flew off the handle, he'd beat Trina up and take out all his anger on her.

Trina finally couldn't take it anymore and just snapped! She waited until Uncle Ronnie fell asleep drunk on the couch. Without saying a word, she had boiled a huge pot of water and walked it over to where he was on the couch. Swooosh!!! She poured out the whole damn hot pot on top of him. "There, bastard!!," she screeched. That afternoon, I had never ever heard anyone scream like a high pitched girl!! Ha, ha, ha. He deserved it!!!

Even though Uncle Ronnie was really hurt pretty badly, Trina took her time calling an ambulance. He managed to scream, "bitch, what the hell?!!" He had to spend weeks in the hospital for severe burns all over his body. My family had asked Trina why she did it and she said, "well, he needed help and maybe by him being in the hospital that he would get the help he needed. Besides, I felt it was payback time!"

When Uncle Ronnie came home from the hospital, things only got worse. He had lost his will to live. His younger brother, Kevin, who also lived in Grandma's house with his wife and two kids, decided to go down to the basement to wash some clothes. We all heard this big scream and then he said, "oh my God, call 911!!" Grandma got scared and wouldn't allow any of us to come down.

Kevin had discovered Uncle Ronnie dead on the floor. He had a drug needle sticking into his penis!! He had taken a drug overdose. The fact that he had stuck the needle into his penis alarmed everybody. Kevin knew he was dead, but tried his best to resuscitate him. He wanted to bring back his big brother. He was in shock and kept saying, "come on Ronnie, wake up, man. Don't do this to me! Don't do this to me!!"

We were all listening upstairs to every single word. I couldn't take anymore death. It was just too much for a young girl like me. Was

God mad at us or something?!! What did we do to deserve this? I was extremely confused and it was growing by the minute.

Uncle Kevin was my favorite uncle. We had the best memories with him. The first time I ever went to the beach or an amusement park was with him. He took Dee and I to many fun places. He was that goofy uncle everyone came to love. Though he did not do drugs or drink like the others, he became very sad and withdrawn. His big brother was gone and that left a hole in his heart. He was never the same again.

He was also Grandma's baby boy. So, he would try and get Dee and I together as much as he could. He knew that it made me sad that Dee and I were apart since she was still living at Aunt Nilsa's house. I decided to stay with him awhile, but I continued to have bad dreams and sometimes, nightmares.

It was too crowded in there, though. Grandma had a big heart and couldn't turn family away. So, it was Grandma, her boyfriend, Uncle Kevin, Trina, and their kids. All crowded in a three bedroom house. I felt cramped and like I had no privacy. I knew it just wasn't the place for me. So, I left.

Unfortunately, I had no choice but to jump from house to house. I was at Grandma, Eve's, Penny's, my cousin Ernestina's, and Aunt Sharon's. I just kept moving, because I was so afraid to wear out my welcome. I dropped out of high school and got two jobs and that's where the real hustle began in my life.

During this crazy time, I met a girl named Keisha, who told me, "I know how we can make one hundred dollars in ten minutes!" Wow, I was floored. I was so excited that I didn't even ask her how and just agreed to sign up with her to make some fast money. She took me way out past Cantonville in a cab to a strange man's house. The job was for us to have sex with this man and he'd pay us that $100.00! What the hell?!!

I went inside of the house with her out of shear curiosity. Once inside, I got really nervous and asked to use the bathroom before getting started. She went with him and automatically began having sex. I broke down in tears. Lord, I don't want to be a prostitute!! What am I doing here! I should have never come with her!

Now, I'm in this strange horny man's bathroom! Ok, this is too much for me. Hell no, I can't do it!! I can't do it!! I began having flashbacks of Jim fondling my breasts for five dollars and almost being raped and killed. What is wrong with me?! God, help me! I don't want to be this prostitute!! I gotta go! I gotta get the hell out of here!!

So, in a panic, I jumped out of the man's bathroom window, which was located on the second floor! At that point, I didn't care. I ran like hell until I saw a bus. I begged the bus driver to let me on. She did. She asked me right away, "what's wrong? Are you ok, kid?" I couldn't answer, because I felt too ashamed. How do I tell her I was almost a prositute?

I put my head down and walked to the back of the bus. I rode that bus for hours not knowing where to go until the bus driver said, "I'm getting off soon. Where do you want to go?" I had no idea where to go, so I decided to go to my cousin Ernestina's house. She was married to a Deacon in their church. I stayed with them for several months. To compensate for me being there, I'd help with their children and around the house.

Unfortunately, one day, Ernestina came home early and found her husband in bed with another woman! All hell broke loose!! Ernestina screamed, "what the hell is going on here?!!" Startled he jumped up and told her, "get out now!!" She was shocked. She had walked in their master bedroom, found him in the bed with another woman, and he wanted her to leave?!! Huh?!!

Was he crazy? The other woman hurried up, grabbed her clothes, and left as fast as she could. Heffer!! After she left, that's when the real fight broke out! He came after Ernestina as if it were all her fault!! He beat her so bad that her left eye closed shut. There was blood all over her face and blouse. She was crying and screaming at the same time. She was traumatized beyond belief. I was frozen and helpless. I was afraid of getting involved after what happened to me at Aunt Nilsa's house. I was petrified and even afraid to go near her.

He had turned everything around on Ernestina and tried to make her feel guilty for not doing more for him. She was slumped down on the floor and holding her face in dire pain. The fight got so bad between them that he even told her, "I don't want Lala here anymore, either!!" I was thinking what the hell did I do? Why do I have to leave? I'm not the one he was in bed with!!

Ernestina wasn't able to do anything and he put me out that day. No warning. Just go. I was stuck for a place to go, so I called my best friend Penny. We were like sisters. We had met in elementary school and remained close. We would share clothes and do each other's hair and if you messed with one of us, you messed with both of us!!! Her mom, Betina, was sympathetic and said, "ok, Lala. I'm going to let you stay for awhile." She actually let me stay about one year, which was more than I even imagined she would.

Penny's father had passed away before she was born. She was raised by her mom, a nurse, who happened to work twelve hour shifts. Sometimes, she would even stay away for a whole weekend to do private duty care case. Penny was very pretty and always attracted boys to her house every time her mom left for work.

So, Penny did pretty much whatever she wanted, because she had no supervison. Sadly, she ended up pregnant by an older guy named Grant, who by the time Penny told him she was pregnant, was in prison for up to ten years for selling drugs. By this time Penny was out of control! Though she was pregnant, she continued to drink and smoke marijuana! Unbelieveable!! I was really mad at her for that.

Later that year, she gave birth two months early, to a baby boy she named Trey. He had to stay in the hospital for several weeks since he was underweight. I'd stare at him through the window where he was in the incubator. He was so tiny and had this little whimper of a cry. We came to visit him everyday. This was all her fault. Had she not been doing drugs and smoking weed, he would have been born healthy. Damn her for this.

I remember thinking if I ever have kids, I won't do that to them. That isn't fair to make a child smoke your cigarettes, drink your booze, and ingest your weed through their blood. Shame on her!!! I never told her how I felt since we were best friends and I was living in her house. I was in survival mode and didn't want to be thrown out of somebody's house again.

Penny had a lot of boyfriends after Trey was born. She was boy crazy! She took full advantage of me being there. She always dropped Trey in my lap every time she wanted to go out with one of them. I know she trusted me with him and it wasn't Trey's fault that his mother was irresponsible. She would come home at all hours of the night and often fell asleep on her way home. Somehow forgetting that she even had a newborn baby waiting for her.

I would even get up in the middle of the night to take care of Trey.

On the days I had to work, I'd come home and find Trey neglected with a dirty pamper and the room smelling like nasty urine. He'd be crying, because not only was he dirty, but very hungry.

I'd reached my breaking point and yelled at her, "what in the hell is wrong with you, Penny?!" She turned around and yelled louder, "what now, Lala?! You don't have to be here either!" What?!!

Every time a disagreement broke out between us, she'd throw that in my face! I hated that about her! This was her baby! She treated me like a live-in babysitter. I was now working at a Donut place and Mexican Take out. She even forced me to take days off and watch Trey when she wanted to just hang out! Damn her!!

I had to take it and take it, because she kept threatening to throw me out every chance she got. Some best friend! She sucked as a friend and she sucked as a mother!

Penny was a horrible sixteen year old mother. If Trey cried, she'd hit and shake him.

Things got so bad between her and Trey. It was as if he knew her energy was bad.

One night, Trey was crying relentlessly. Penny freaked out and grabbed him out of his bed, put him in the bathtub and turned the hot water on him! Oh Lord, poor little Trey started screaming. I came running in the bathroom and snatched Trey out of her hands. I said, "what the hell are you doing? Are you trying to kill him?"

She turned on me with this evil face and snarled, "I hate that little crying bitch! He ruined my life!!" She was out of control and ran out of the house. I instantly ran to call her mom, Betina. Enough was enough! Betina was in shock and tried to comfort me by saying, "I'm on my way home, please keep Trey with you until I get there." I assured her I would and locked the front door so Penny couldn't come in.

I took Trey to the sink and tried to pour cool water on his hot burns. After Betina arrived, we got Trey dressed and rushed to the hospital. His tender skin was really red and I knew it wasn't good. Once we got to the hospital, the doctors took Trey and then asked Betina and I to go into this little side room. Betina knew why, but I didn't. So, Betina explained to me, "Lala, Trey was abused by his mother. They intend to get to the bottom of this. Stay calm and let me do the talking."

I nodded yes and then put my head on her shoulder. I couldn't believe

Penny did that to Trey. She's so dumb hurting a helpless baby like that! The hospital staff decided to keep Trey and turn him over to the custody of Department of Social Services. Penny was furious that we reported what happened, especially me. She took it all out on me.

She accused me of being jealous of her and wanting to destroy her life! She's so stupid. How could I ever be jealous of a bad mother? I got so tired of her blaming me for the whole thing that I came up with the idea to leave the house.

Chapter Four
Survival Mode...

I decided to have a heart to heart with Betina. I asked her, "Betina, can you sign me up for the Job Corps on your next day off?" Since I was only sixteen, I needed an adult's consent to get into the program. So, she did. She knew and understood what I was going through with Penny. She also felt like I had had enough and something had to give.

Everything was set and I was on my way to the Job Corps, just like that!

I went off to the Job Corps, where I received my high school diploma and certified nursing assistant certification, the step before Nursing School. While I was attending the program, my dad, Dee, and Aunt Nilsa would write to me and I would eagerly write them back. During Thanksgiving Holiday, that year, Aunt Nilsa surprised me and sent me a round-trip bus ticket to come and spend the holiday with the family. I was really excited, because I hadn't seen Dee for a long while.

Seeing Dee brought back old memories and I really missed her. When I got off the bus, everyone was awaiting me. Dee ran right up to me. She had gotten so big that I almost didn't even recognize her. She jumped on me and practically knocked me down. "Lala, I missed you," she exclaimed. It made me happy to return. Thanksgiving was great as long as I was just visiting.

I then completed the one-year program in Charleston, West Virginia. Charleston was an extremely racist town back then. I was so light that white people didn't know whether to accept me or not, but the black students called me, "mutt," "mixed breed," or "half-n-half." I moved back to Maryland with several thousand dollars saved up. Aunt Sharon had secured a job for me babysitting two children of the woman she did house work for. I was able to save even more money than ever before.

I was lucky to land a live-in babysitter job for the pitcher of the Baltimore Orioles! Unfortunately, he ended up being traded from the Orioles. So, I got my first apartment in Baltimore County and was excited to furnish the whole thing. Although I was having fun doing that, I felt lonely and sad. No mother, a father in prison, and my only sister living far away at Aunt Nilsa's house.

My first nursing job was at Inns of Evergreen Nursing and Rehab. After a few months of working there, I was back in school to get my nursing license. Penny and I had totally stopped speaking. I heard from mutual friends that she had dropped out of school, had another baby, and was even more heavy into drugs.

I felt sad for her, but since she was so mean to me, I felt I should just leave her alone and not look back . There was just no talking to her. She was bullheaded and high all the time. I was moving in a new direction and she turned out to be a lousy friend. I know she would only try and mess things up for me. I didn't need that negativity in my life anymore. I was moving on.

I submerged myself in work and tried to block out the past. A year had passed that quick. I was now eighteen and I met an older man named Edward. He was twenty six. The Jazz girl, whose house I was at when my mother died, introduced me to him. She had moved into the same apartment houses that I had moved into in Essex, Md. She was also dating Edward's best friend at the time. Edward would come over to my apartment all the time. We'd watch movies and have long talks.

I didn't know much about him. Only that he seemed like a nice guy to spend time with. I never smoked or did any drugs and neither did he at the time. The first time Edward and I had sex, it was very intense. I now felt more like a woman. I had my own place and my own man. I was really floating on air.

The second time Edward and I had sex, I got pregnant! Just that quick! I found out I was having a son. A son. My very own son! Whewhewww, no more lonely days! I was happy and thought this was a gift from God. I would have someone to love and someone who would love me back. The sadness was over. No more lonely days. All of the girls I grew up with were having kids at fifteen and sixteen years old.

I was thrilled that I had waited until I was eighteen to have kids. I was proud of myself that I had gone back to school to become a licensed practical nurse. I had done it! But, when I told Edward about the pregnancy, he froze. He looked like he had seen a ghost. He looked at me and said, "I don't want anymore children, Lala." I was shocked. I didn't know he had any children!

Apparently Edward had several women. One of them was already pregnant and due two months before I was! Oh Lord, I can't believe him! What a pig! I thought I was his only girl! He had numerous children all over the damn place. What a whore! I guess I was so lonely that I held on to the first man that paid me any attention. After finding out about all that, I still decided to keep my son, but get rid of Edward.

Edward was pressuring me to have an abortion. So, just to please him, I made the appointment for the abortion. But, on the day I was suppose to have it, I couldn't go through with it. I wanted my son. It was my body and my baby. I was so angry at Edward for trying to push me into that that I resented him greatly.

Edward finally came around and accepted my pregnancy. There was nothing he could do about it. I was fiercely determined to have my son. I wondered about the other girl he got pregnant, but it made me mad and every time I looked at him I tried to imagine him with her. It infuriated me. He was seeing both of us at the same time. That really pissed me off. I would curse him out every time we got into a fight about it.

He knew I cared about him. Why did he even need her when he had a good woman like me? I'd ask him from time to time if he was still with her and he refused to answer me, which made me even more upset at him.

To pacify me, Edward would come over and stay on the weekends. During the week, he supposedly stayed at his mother's house. She lived in a rough part of South Baltimore in these row of houses near Monroe Street. I doubted that's where he was, because of the other woman who was pregnant. So, we'd argue about it all the time.

By this time, my dad was out of prison and on a work release program. I was so happy to have him home. He would often visit me and spend weekends at my apartment. He met a much younger woman, my age, called Fran. They fell in love quickly and she got pregnant. She was also studying to become a nurse like me. So, we had a lot in common.

I felt conflicted about the whole thing. I kept wishing mom was still alive and that they'd still be together now. I tried to be happy for my dad and I understood that it wasn't Fran's fault about all this. So, I gave him my blessing and welcomed her into my life. After all, it was his life and not my decision to make. My father seemed so happy, too. But, I couldn't help thinking in the back of my mind that Fran was having the life my mom was never able to have.

I was now nine months pregnant and going into labor. It was a Saturday October 15, 1988 and it was my day off of work. I remember eating breakfast and watching cartoons. I was all alone in the apartment when my water broke! I didn't have a car, so I had to call a cab. When the cab arrived, a sweet guy got out. He said his name was Mark. I told him I was in labor. He put plastic over the seats and helped me in. I will never forget him, because he made me laugh all the way to the hospital. He chuckled, "Lala, girl, you better not have that baby in this cab!"

Thankfully I didn't. We made it to the hospital in time. As we pulled up to the Emergency Room, I was met by my doctor and he immediately hooked me up to this labor monitor. After more than eighteen hours in labor, my doctor came in and told me that the baby is in danger and I had to have a C-Section to get him out or he could die. I agreed to do it, but I was so scared. Where was Edward?!

I found out that my family members had started showing up. Dee had been with me all day with this worried look on her face, which made me more nervous. My favorite cousin, Racine had arrived with Maureen, who was one of our cousin's wives. Racine came into my room and asked me, "where is Edward? He's the father. He should be here even if you guys are having problems." I was thinking, I know right?!

I reluctantly explained to her that I had called his mother's house and she said, "I tried to call Edward, but Lala, I couldn't reach him." It was time for me to go into the operating room. I was so scared and nervous that I started to pray, "dear Lord, please let everything go ok. It's in your hands now, amen." Finally, Shawn was born. He did not cry. In fact, he was blue! So, the nurses rushed him out of the room and I automatically started to cry.

I was praying out loud now, "please God, don't take my baby from me. He is all I have." Dee and Racine were hugging me and telling me everything is going to be ok. I knew that was a lie. Why was he blue? Is he dead!? Ten long minutes later my doctor came from the NICU where Shawn now was and said, "Shawn's lungs were filled with a fluid called conium, but we got him to breathe on his own." Oh, thank you Lord!! I went from being totally sad to being the happiest woman alive!

Shawn was five pounds, nine ounces. They had put him in an incubator with lights and wires coming out of him. The nurse had an oxygen mask over his face. They rushed me in quickly so that I could put my hand inside of the incubator and touch him. I did. His skin was so soft and he was so tiny. He looked cold and his little lips were quivering. So, tears filled my eyes and I said, "mommy is her Shawn. Mommy is here, baby." Then they carted him off to the NICU for more observation and care.

Edward finally showed up, but he was drunk! I could smell the liquor on his breath from across the room. Oddly, no one in his family showed up. They didn't seem to like me much and didn't want Edward to have a child with me. I didn't really know them either, so we were even. Edward asked me, "Lala, can you give Shawn my last name, because I have all girls and no boys to carry my name." Look at that. His family barely wanted to have anything to do with me and I was the one that gave him his first son!

Going against my better judgment, I agreed to give Shawn his last name. My dad had already told me to give Shawn our last name, because he felt that there was no future between Edward and I. Father knew best. He thought that Edward was playing me and he would eventually leave me. It made me sad, but I had to admit that it is what it is.

Dad was so intelligent. After spending almost his whole life in prison, he had gotten his GED. He also did College classes and earned two degrees! He was really trying to be a better man. I made myself a promise that I would never again smoke, do drugs, or drink alcohol. I was determined to be the best mom ever, especially with my dad by my side.

Edward was coming to stay at my house more and more. He was really starting to get on my nerves! One day, he came to my house drunk as hell! He ranted until he was fighting with me for no reason. He tried to make up with me by saying, "don't be mad," as he bent over to try and kiss me. I shoved him away, because I never could stand the smell of alcohol. I had the baby in my arms and he reacted as if he didn't care.

He punched me dead in my face! Oh Lord, the baby fell on the floor!! I was furious!!

I went into an absolute rage, "what the hell, Edward, are you crazy!!" I bent down and picked up the baby. His gums were bleeding and he was balling tears. This son of a bitch is going to pay for that! I gathered myself well enough to put the baby in the crib. Then I went off!!!!!

First, I grabbed a chair and hurled it at him!! I was so vexed that I began hauling the broom, shoes, and anything else I could to hurt him. He did his best to stay away from me at this point, because he knew that I could go off. Some next door neighbor heard what was going on and called the police.

When the police arrived, they came to the door. I answered. They were shocked when they saw me with a purple bruise on my face and when they looked at Edward, he was bleeding. They arrested him on the spot and charged me with disturbance. Trust me, I am not a violent person, but when the baby fell on the floor, I just lost it. I had seen too much abuse in my life and was damned if I was going to stand for that!

That was the end of our relationship as a couple. I didn't want to end up like my mother or other family members, physically and mentally abused. So, as much as possible, I was determined not to let Shawn out of my sight. I went to work everyday and he was attending a Christian Daycare. I would go and pick him up right after work. I was not your average nineteen year old. I didn't party or go out with my friends. I just wanted to be a good mother.

I was still in nursing school to further my nursing career. It was so hard to work, go to school and then pick up Shawn from the day care. I didn't even have a car. So, by this time, the bus driver, knew me by name and we became friends. One night, after working my shift that night from 3-11pm, I picked up Shawn and dashed home to get some rest. I was really exhausted that day.

Around 2:00am, I heard someone banging on my door like a lunatic. It was Edward. He screamed out, "Yo, Lala!! Lala!! I want to see Shawn!! Is he crazy?!!! It's the middle of the night for God's sake!! He had been drinking much more than usual. I opened the door just to shut him up. He pushed passed me and came in without me even giving him permission.

He lied when he said that he only wanted to see Shawn. He wanted to have sex. He didn't even go to Shawn first. He made a bee line for me. His breath was so gross. It smelled like a combination of cigarettes and alcohol. So disgusting, that I had to hold my breath. He forced me onto the bed and pulled my panties down. I began kicking and screaming until he overpowered me.

He was so drunk that he couldn't get it up. He was struggling to get it in while I was trying to fight him off of me. He slurred, what sounded like, "you're gonna give me some sex, bitch." I was mortified. I knew I had to do something. Something big and this time I was going for it!

He kept slobbering kisses on my face while I was resisting him. I'm gonna make him pay for trying to rape me like this! He kept trying to hump on me without an erection. Shawn was now crying with all the commotion.

He was too strong on me. So, I waited for him to exhaust his damn self and then I made my move. He finally passed out on me. I went into the kitchen, got a kitchen knife and a pot of cold water. I poured the cold water on him and he immediately jumped up. He gargled, "Lala, what the hell are you doing?!" I came back with, "getting rid of your drunk ass!!" I pulled the knife on him and said, "Edward, I want you out of my damn house, now!!"

He refused and we started to fight and went at it blow for blow. When he got a good punch in and hit me in the face, I couldn't take it anymore and stabbed him in the head! Only the tip of the knife went in, but he was screaming like crazy. He reacted by slapping me in the face, and then he punched me. I started kicking, biting, and scratching his face all up.

That got him scared. Standing there with the knife in his head. He pulled it out, threw it on the floor, and then left. The next morning, his mother called me right up. She was angry at me and said, "Lala, why the hell did you stab him in the head and screw up his face?!" I was so pissed. I told her, "go ask your son what he did to me last night. How he tried to rape me, and he kept punching me in the face!"

She always hated me, because she thought I was too young for her son to begin with and never wanted me to have Shawn. She actually wanted me to have an abortion. Dumb heffer!! Who the hell was she to tell me what to do with my precious body? I had my son and he's beautiful. I don't give a rat's ass what she thinks. The feeling was mutual. She could go to hell, too.

Edward was a real mama's boy! He lived in his mother's basement. One of his cousins, that also lived there, told me Edward was now heavier into drugs and drinking. He could never hold down a job. So, I never received any child support from him. His mother, however, would sometimes buy a gift and bring to Shawn. But, most times, she would tell me, "I bought this for Shawn, but it has to stay at my house for when he comes over." That didn't make no damn sense.

I resolved myself to the fact that it was just going to be Shawn and I. Because of the bad experience I had had with Edward, I was afraid to have any men around me. Fate intervened again and while Shawn and I were shopping in Golden Ring Mall, I met a guy named Hank. He was good looking, too.

Hank was very sweet. The total opposite of Edward. He was kind and thoughtful. He was very good to Shawn and I, which made it so easy to like him. I wasn't even looking for someone, because Edward and I had just broken up three months earlier. Hank treated Shawn like he was his real father. I was impressed.

He would come over all the time and bring pampers and new clothes for Shawn. He took me to the movies, dinners, and fairs!! It made me wish he were Shawn's real father.

Hank never cursed at me or lost his temper. He was a gentleman. He'd even hold car doors open for me. I was so thrilled. Finally a good man!!! He taught me how to drive. He and I became very close. He would do anything for me, but I was too afraid to fall in love this time.

Shortly after, I ended up getting pregnant by Hank. When I told him I was pregnant, he was so happy, but I was scared and confused. I didn't know if I wanted to have more children without being married and trying to finish nursing school. I was already a single mother, working and trying to stay in school. So, I told Hank, "this isn't a good time for me to be having more children." He disagreed and pleaded with me to change my mind.

Shawn was now fifteen months old and I told Hank that I didn't want to be a "baby mama" again. Hank cried and said, "I love you so much, Lala. I want to take care of you, Shawn, and our new baby." He even told me he would one day make me his wife. I knew he would make a great father and husband, but I just wasn't ready. I prayed to God for guidance and forgiveness.

It broke my heart, but my mind was made up. I decided to end the pregnancy. I knew that abortion was wrong, but I also believed that you should never bring a baby into the world that you can't afford to take care of. I felt that was also wrong.

Part of the reason I decided not to have the baby was because I had a feeling that Hank was out selling drugs. He never went to work, but always had money on him and two expensive cars, a Corvette and a Volvo. As much as I liked Hank and the attention he showed me and my son, I was not in love with him. I had to put Shawn first and so I ended the relationship between Hank and myself.

Months had passed and Edward finally got back in touch with me. He said, "me and my family want to see Shawn." His mother then took the phone and said, "we all want to see him, Lala." Though I was somewhat skeptical, I agreed. He hadn't seen Shawn for so long. I knew how it felt to grow up without a father in my home and I wanted Shawn to know his father.

So, after I got off of work one Friday, I decided to take Shawn to Edward's family house for the weekend. I kissed Shawn and hugged him and told him, "mommy will be back on Sunday for you. I love you, baby." As I started to leave, Shawn began to cry and so did I. I cried the whole way home. My car was in the shop getting repaired, because the alternator needed to be changed. So, I had to take a one hour bus ride back to Baltimore County from the City.

When I got home, I was still crying. I missed Shawn a lot. I went inside the house and called them right away to check on Shawn. They said he was all right and had stopped crying. I knew it was true, because I could hear him laughing in the backround.

Edward got on the phone and said, "he's fine, Lala." I hung up, but I was still so sad. My apartment felt so empty without Shawn there. I grabbed one of Shawn's favorite toys and cried myself to sleep in his room.

That Saturday, I went to work for 3-11pm shift. About 6:00pm, I received a frantic phone call. It was one of Edwards' cousins saying, "Lala, Edward has been shot and he had Shawn with him." I screamed and slammed down the phone. I told my boss what happened and left right away in a cab. I was freaking out!! Was Shawn shot, too?!! What happened?!! I couldn't get there fast enough.

My heart was pounding so fast that I thought it would explode. As I approached Edward's house, I was crying hysterically. I was greeted by his cousin Renee. She was holding Shawn in her arms and he appeared to be okay. He lit up when he saw me and smiled with his six little teeth in his mouth. He yelled, "mommy, mommy!!" I snatched him out of her arms and held his little body next to mine.

It was a relief that he was all right. My heart started to calm down. I checked Shawn all over his body to make sure he hadn't been shot. I then turned my attention to Renee and asked her, " what's wrong? Why did you say Shawn was shot? Where's Edward?" She looked at me and said, "Lala, that's not what I said. I told you Edward was shot and that Shawn was with him. You hung up the phone before I could finish explaining everything to you."

"I'm so sorry," I said. "I freaked out. I thought something happened to Shawn. He's my life. He's all I have, Renee. I can't lose him, too." I asked, " why was Edward shot?" She said, "Edward owed someone money for drugs he had gotten from them earlier in the week and he never paid them. So, when they saw Edward walking down the street with Shawn, they shot him. Edward had been shot four times in the stomach and once in the groin.

I said, "what drugs? I didn't know Edward was still on drugs!" Why the hell would he be walking over there with my eighteen month old son in his arms?!! Damn him!! Shawn could have been killed!! His dumb ass went to the corner store on a Saturday night to buy some freaking beer!

Even though I was seeing red, I asked her did Edward make it. She replied, "I don't know yet. He was rushed to the hospital. The paramedics had worked on him for twenty minutes to stabilize him before he was brought to Maryland's Shock Trauma Center. Out of concern, I took a cab with Shawn and headed for the hospital. I was told he was going to make it, but he might be paralyzed from the waist down. I went to see him. He was lying in intensive care with all these tubes and breathing machines. In that instant, all I could think about was Shawn. I said to myself that this is not the life I want for him. From that moment on, I knew this wasn't the life I would allow Shawn to become accustomed to.

I promised myself that I would not let Shawn grow up in the same environment that Edward did. So, I decided to take drastic action. I moved, got a new job, and not let Edward know where I moved to. I didn't want to keep Edward and Shawn apart, but I had no choice. I just wanted the best for my child. I never actually knew anything about Edward. He was just someone for me to spend time with. I got pregnant before we even had a chance to know each other.

We never went out. Not even to a movie or anything. It was just sex and companionship. It didn't even feel like a relationship. He'd come over, we'd have sex, talk a bit, and he'd leave. Nothing deep at all. We never got close.

I was taking birth control pills, but they failed me. That's why I believe Shawn was meant to be. My mother had died and God sent me a son. Soon after, I had a couple of really nice male friends, but none with whom I wanted to spend the rest of my life with. Hank would still come around, even though we were just friends now. He knew I was alone. I couldn't stop him from calling or coming around, because he still loved me. I didn't want to be cold since he had been so nice to Shawn and I.

He even had the nerve to confront Edward and tell him that he loved Shawn and I and that he intended to be there for us. Which didn't go over well with Edward. I never asked what happened between them, because I just didn't want to know.

After years of being apart from me, Dee had started to visit Shawn and I. She was still living with Aunt Nilsa and going to school. We began to start getting close again. I would often ask her questions about our childhood, but she didn't seem to remember anything. She had managed to block out everything and she even got mad when I'd bring up the past in front of her.

I had finally finished the nursing program and the only thing left for me to do was take my boards. I took the test, but didn't pass them. So, I was a little discouraged. I chose to concentrate on my son and work hard. I was hoping that at some point I would go back and retake my exams. I decided to take a six month course to become a medical assistant. I completed that and got certified.

One Saturday, Dee and I had spent the day together driving around town. We went to Inner Harbor. Just before going to the movies, I met this guy named John. He seemed like a nice guy. He had this light brown skin, medium build, black wavy hair, and a beautiful smile. He was also very shy. He seemed like just an average guy working at one of the largest hotels in downtown Baltimore. He worked in the supply room.

He walked up to me and said, "hi, I'm John, can I have your phone number." I hesitated for a minute, because I wasn't sure I was ready for dating. I looked over at Dee and she nodded her head yes. I took her advice and we exchanged numbers.

From that day on, John and I talked every day. Sometimes, we spoke for hours at a time. We could talk about everything, including his ex-girlfriends, my exes, and all the things we had both experienced. We would, at times, even fall asleep while on the phone and when I woke up, John would still be on the other end!!

We then started going to the movies and dinners and spending time together. It was almost too good to be true, but it was. John was always everything I ever wanted in a man. He got along so well with my son. He took me to meet his parents, John Sr. and his mom Gloria, and his brother, Jack. They lived on the East Side of Baltimore in a row of houses that they were renting. They were so wonderful to Shawn and I.

We would go to John's mother's house every Sunday for dinner and if we missed one Sunday, she would fuss at us, "why didn't you bring my baby, Shawn, over here to see us?!" He was the only grandchild they got to see. Jack had a daughter when he was still in high school, but the mother of that child had moved on and gotten married. Her new husband didn't want him coming around. So, he rarely got to see his daughter let alone anybody else.

One day, out of the blue, Hank called me. I told him, "Hank, I've met someone new and I don't think you should call me anymore." He said, " Lala, I'm heart broken, but I will always love you and Shawn." He told me that he had some things he had bought for Shawn and wanted to bring them to me. I felt so bad, because Hank had always been so good to us. Yet, I had made my decision and I had to stick with it.

I decided to tell John about Hank's call and he agreed that I had made the right choice. We talked it over and changed my phone number so Hank couldn't call me anymore. John and I became very close. We shared everything. We'd go out for dinner and a movie every single weekend and we'd make dinners at home together. I had never felt a bond like this with anyone before.

We became the best of friends long before we ever had sex and that was a good thing. It was the next natural to step to our friendship. Later that year, John asked me to marry him!! I couldn't believe it. I said, "John, are you sure you want to marry me when I already have a child by another man?" He laughed and said, "yes, of course I do. Lala, I love you." My eyes welled up with tears as I hugged him and told him, "yes, yes, yes!! I'll marry you!! John, I love you, too."

Hank called me after he managed to get my new phone number from one of my aunt's that liked him. I told him I was engaged to John and he asked me if he could atleast say goodbye to Shawn. As much as it hurt me, I told him that I thought that it was a bad idea. I felt it would show disrespect to John. I was not about to allow anything to come between us. I had never experienced true love before, but I could feel just how much John loved me and the feeling was mutual. So, I told Hank no.

Chapter Five
Moving On…

John and I had grown incredibly close and decided to schedule our wedding day for August 21, 1992. We started making plans quite quickly. Some of our family and friends thought we were moving way too fast and that we weren't going to make it. We ignored everyone of them and followed our hearts. We drew even closer each other every time someone doubted our love and commitment to one another.

We paid for the wedding ourselves with the help of my father, who bought my wedding dress and John's parents, who paid for the photographer. My father and John got along so well. I think it made my dad really happy that John had asked my dad for his blessing. Thankfully, John did not smoke or do any drugs, which made my dad proud. Dad was over excited that he even bought me a fifteen hundred dollar wedding gown!! I was shocked, but deeply touched and very happy.

During the time we were planning for the wedding, about three months in, I found out I was pregnant with John's first child. I was confused, because I knew we had been using condoms most of the time. I know that we took a chance by being lazy and not using the condoms all the time, but we loved each other and really didn't expect anything to happen that soon. I loved John so much and wanted to be his wife, but I wanted everything to be perfect.

I didn't want to walk down the aisle pregnant, so I suggested to John that maybe this baby was coming too soon and I should end the pregnancy. He looked at me straight in the eyes and said, "Lala, no. I love you and I want you to have my baby. We'll just move up the wedding date." I was relieved, because I didn't want to have an abortion. I just thought things were moving faster than I expected. It was one thing to plan our wedding within a year, but a baby would take even bigger planning.

I trusted John and put it in God's hands. John and I set out to find a Pastor and a Church to marry us. We met a very nice Pastor named Pastor Florence who belonged to small, but nice Church called The Open Bible Baptiste Church on the East Side of Baltimore County.

Pastor Florence stated, "I can only marry you both if you attend my marriage counseling sessions for one month." We agreed. The Pastor then said, "I want to make sure that the you young people understand what you are getting into. This is a life long commitment." He went on to explain that he didn't believe in divorces. He told us that he wanted us to be absolutely sure that we wanted to be together forever. We decided not to tell him that I was pregnant.

We just didn't want him to assume that that was the reason John and I were getting married. After our counseling sessions were over, we went on with the formal wedding plans. We moved up the wedding date to March 21, 1992. Five months earlier. By the time we were ready to say I do, I was now five months pregnant.

The day of the wedding came and when we got married, I felt like the good year blimp!! John and his groomsmen had already arrived in a white limo. Shortly after, my limo arrived with my bridesmaids. God, I was so happy and nervous all at once! It felt like my heart had dropped down into my stomach. My Aunt Sharon had come in and rushed back where I was waiting for the ceremony to begin.

She looked at me with tear filled eyes and said, "girl, your mother would be so proud of you." She said I looked so beautiful and that she couldn't believe her eyes. I couldn't keep it together after that and broke down and started crying uncontrollably. I started to reminisce about my mother and all the things I had gone through to get to this day, which, by the way, I thought I'd never see.

My father walked in just in time to hug me and tell me, "Lala, you're going to be okay. Stay strong. This is your wedding day." My make-up had run all over my face. I was a mess. Thank God I had invited my Avon representative to the wedding! She came in so handy, for real!! She had already done the make-up job on me and I screwed it up by crying. Little did I know she'd have to redo it again.

The song I chose to walk down the aisle to was "Always," by Atlantic

Star and when it began to play, it was time for me to make my grand entrance. My father looked at me just before we began our walk and said, "Lala, I am so proud of you and you look beautiful." He kissed me on my cheek and asked, "are you ready, baby girl?" I looked over at him and said, "yes, Daddy. I'm ready." The Usher opened the doors of the Sanctuary and I locked eyes on John. He looked so handsome!!!

I'll never forget the way he was looking at me. It made me feel like Cinderella. Although the Church was small and we had only seventy five guests, it felt like forever walking down that aisle. Everyone was starring at me and camera flashes were going off. After my father walked me down the aisle, he hugged John and then put John's hand in mine. John turned to me and said, "baby, you look so beautiful. I can't believe you're going to be my wife." Right then, my heart melted, and I was no longer nervous. I knew this was where I was supposed to be.

Dee was one of my bridesmaids. The only person missing was my mother, who still had an empty seat reserved in the front row. I wanted to acknowledge her even though she was gone. Next to her sitting there was Aunt Nilsa, who did her best to act in my mom's place. She was just sitting there with the biggest smile on her face.

Aunt Nilsa and I were close again. She no longer smoked or drank and she was treating me more as if I were one of her own daughters. My wedding had turned out to be like a fairy tale. I had my Prince John and he truly rescued me from a life of loneliness and despair. I now felt safe and even though John didn't have any money or a good job lined up yet, none of that mattered to me as much as having his love in my life.

I had married into a whole new family, who had accepted Shawn and I as their own. I had told them how much family meant to me since I had literally grown up without my own. In my childhood, I never had a birthday party, or was taken to the Zoo, nor the movies, or any amusement parks. I never attended any Church with my parents or even sat at a table to have a simple family dinner. Sadly, those were things I only saw families do on T.V.

After the wedding, John and I went to D.C. for a short honeymoon with very little money. We promised each other that we would make up for it later on down the road, because we had a baby on the way and we didn't want to spend unnecessary money. We knew we loved each other and all we wanted to do was get married and we did.

I worked very hard at being a good wife and mother. On August 31st , 1992, I gave birth to my second son, John Jr. My husband was by my side the whole time and so was his mother Gloria. Even Dee came to be with me. I was really starting to feel whole. I felt so much love in that room that day. I just had wished my mom could have been there to meet her new grandson, but I knew she was there in spirit.

Believe it or not, shortly after John Jr. was born, I became pregnant again. Less than a year had passed and on Thanksgiving Day, we had another son, Jason, whom we called J.J. for short. Believe me, I was incredibly thankful to God. I now had three sons!!! Dee was also now pregnant and five months later, Dee had her first son, whom she named Drake.

I was right by her side when my nephew came into the world. Drake's dad, Marc, was Dee's on-again, off-again boyfriend. When Drake was born, it was one of their off times. So, Marc never even came to the hospital to see his son being born. I could see the sadness in Dee's eyes. I knew she felt alone. I was so happy to be there and share that tender moment with her. John and our three sons sat in the lobby waiting for me to come down.

I thought about them as I was coming down the elevator. I had a husband who loved and adored me and three beautiful sons that loved and needed me. I felt a real sense of purpose. I prayed that Dee would find someone else to love and also love her back. I still felt very over protective of her and would often call Marc and fuss at him for the way he mistreated her. She was so crazy about him that she wouldn't entertain any notion of dating another man. She would sit around and wait for Marc instead.

I was so pissed off at him that I told him to leave my sister the hell alone. He bit back with, "Lala, mind your business!!" I snapped back, "this is my life and Dee is my damn business!!" He walked away defeated by my words and was speechless. That snake knew I was right and I didn't have a problem telling him so. Bastard!!

Dee's situation made me think of my own. Could I get any luckier than how things were? Can my life get any better for me? So, I stopped and thanked God for everything I now had, "God, you have blessed me with a loving husband and three sons. I love you and I thank you for all of it."

Yet and still, I would sometimes reflect on my past and break down and cry feeling sorry for myself for the lousy cards I had been dealt. How my mother never will get a chance to meet her beautiful grandchildren, how Dee was still a single mother and living at Aunt Nilsa's house, and how my father was now sent back to prison after he had made so much progress with a fiancee and a new baby.

A man, whom my father didn't even know, was also in the same pre-release program that my father had been in, went into a jealous rage, shot his girlfriend, and then shot himself. So, based on his case, the government took away the pre-release program and ordered everyone released early back to jail to serve their time. Unfortunately, my dad was one of them.

All the progress and hard work that my father had done seemed to be in vain. They ignored that and sent him back to prison. No exceptions. No mercy. My father had been in jail since he was seventeen. He was so sad. He didn't want to go back and I didn't blame him. He was recommended and up for parole more than once, but the Governor of Maryland wouldn't sign the papers for his parole release.

Meanwhile, I was happily married to John for five years now, when Edward finally tracked me down. Guess he didn't die that night he had been shot. He found out where I worked from one of his relatives who came into the Emergency Room of the local hopsital I was working in and secretly spotted me.

One day, I got a frantic call from one of my co-workers who said, "Lala, you'd better come quick. There's a man here screaming and claiming he knows you and wants you to come down immediately." I knew it was him, because as I made my way downstairs, I could hear his crazy ass voice, "Lala, get down here. I want to see my damn son! You here me, bitch?!"

I came around the corner and Edward had this really sick look in his eyes as if he wanted to kill me. I knew I had to do something. I went home and told John everything. He suggested we go and talk to an attorney to see how we could find a way to keep Edward out of our lives for good. The attorney told us that the only thing we could do is take Edward to court and sue him for custody with no visitation rights.

The attorney also warned that the Judge could give Edward a chance to get a job, pay child support, and get his life together, too. A consideration the Judge may make since Edward had not seen Shawn for many years now. So, I immediately began to pray and ask God for guidance and strength.

In good faith, I decided to make arrangements for Shawn to spend the weekend with his father. I felt it was time to try and make peace with Edward for Shawn's sake. John and I, along with our two sons, dropped Shawn off together that Friday. I could tell by the look on John's face that he was going along with it, but he didn't seem happy at all.

He disagreed with the decision, but he was very supportive of me and trusted my judgment call. It was the longest weekend of our lives. We missed Shawn terribly and wondered how he was doing in Edwards' care. Sunday finally came and we all set out to pick Shawn up. When we got there, Shawn looked at us, got in the car, and never uttered a word. It was like he was mad at us for leaving him there. I felt so guilty. It had scarred him and he wasn't his talkative self.

So, I tried to engage Shawn in conversation by saying, "what is wrong, honey? Did someone hurt you? Tell mommy the truth. I won't let anyone hurt you, baby." Shawn was apprehensive at first, but then he whispered, "mom, he didn't feed me." I almost burst into tears, but held them back and replied, "what do you mean he didn't feed you, Shawn?" Shawn was only eight years old and very used to our way of living.

He excitedly said, "Mommy, the spending money you gave me, he took and spent it on cigarettes and beer. He only bought me penny candy with the change they gave him. He made me stay in a room with no T.V. and no games. When I came out to tell him I was hungry, he said he was busy sitting in the living room with one of his friends. They had some white sugar on a mirror and were sniffing it up with a rolled up dollar bill."

As I was listening to Shawn, my eyes filled with huge tears. Memories of my childhood flooded my mind and began to haunt me again. Damn it. I reached for Shawn, who was sitting in the back seat of the car, and hugged him as tight as I could. I felt as if I had let him down by bringing him to see his drug addicted father. I promised him that I would protect him and never let this happen again.

That night, I layed awake crying thinking about all the ways I had to find to keep my son safe. Then, out of the blue, it hit me. I knew exactly what I was going to do!! The next day, I called my job and told them I wasn't going to be able to come in. I set out to find a house fifty miles away from the house we were living in.

John and I agreed to find something fast and move by the end of the month. A short time after, I lost my job at the hospital, where I had been working in the ER. I had worked there more than three years. My supervisor and I had a great working relationship, but she stated that she couldn't allow Edward to cause so much turmoil in the work place. Shawn's father had been coming there constantly drunk and high asking for Shawn.

I understood her sentiment. After all, people came to the hospital to feel better not get caught up in my private family drama. I ended up getting a new job at a hospital closer to our new home, which was more convenient for me and Edward didn't know where we were now, which made me feel so relieved and safer.

Fate finally interviened. Several months later, I found out from Edward's cousin, Renee, that Edward had been arrested for burglary and attempted robbery and was possibly facing ten years in prison.

While at my new job, I met a nurse named Richie. He often came to the hospital regarding his patients. He said he liked my outgoing personality and had a job proposition for me. I was intrigued. He said that he owned a Nursing Agency and could use a new Nurse Manager. I would be in charge of all the nurses. The best part, he said he'd double my salary!! Who could turn that down?! I jumped at the offer!!

When I started working for Richie, I met a nurse named Sofia. We became close very quickly and started hanging out. We'd take our lunch breaks together. We began talking a lot. Richie's agency only employed critical care nurses. So, after two years of working for him, I came to him with an excellent idea. I asked him if we could talk for a bit. He said, "sure, Lala. Come in and close the door."

I told him we should expand the business by hiring certified nursing assistants and LPN nurses. I was aware of the high demand for LPN's, because I had gone through the program. Many LPN's were looking to work for private agencies, because they paid much better than hospitals. Richie loved the idea. He said, "if you can make that happen, Lala, I'll give you ten percent of the company!" What?! Is he serious?!! Whewhewww!!

I was ecstatic.

As I knew it would be, my idea was a booming success! Richie was extremely happy with the business and how it was progressing. So, I was bold enough to hold him to his promise and asked him when I'd get the ten percent of the shares signed over to me. All he kept saying from time to time was, "soon, Lala, soon." One year passed and that soon never came! Tension started to mount between us in the office and I was getting really turned off.

After having J.J., John and I had decided that I would have my tubes tied since we didn't want to have anymore children. Boy, were we wrong!! We had had a real change of heart. Though we had three beautiful sons, John and I longed for a daughter. We chose to have a tubal reversal so that we could try for a girl. We made plans to see a fertility doctor and schedule the procedure.

While in the hospital, I received a call from one of my employees, Karen, who informed me that she overheard Richie saying to Earl, one of his partners, that he was thinking of letting me go! What?!!

The next day, Richie called me and confirmed the rumor. He said he had to let me go, because of the tension and attitude I had toward him. I told him, "Richie, I don't have an attitude. I just want what you promised me since last year. Ten percent of the shares like you said. I'm hurt, because you lied to me and strung me along for more than a year. I doubled your profits in this last year. I held up to my end of the deal, but you didn't come through on yours."

I further added, "as a matter of fact, because of what I did for your business, you had the ability to buy new cars and a two and a half million dollar house in Boca Raton, Florida! On the water, no less! And for that, I never got anything extra?" He never said a thing and just hung up the phone on me! I was so mad and called him right back. I informed him that because of his greed, he would never be truly blessed.

I lastly said, "God will take care of you and I pray that God will have mercy on your soul. You are driven by greed and trust me, it will be your downfall!" Then I hung up on him! It made me so mad. What was wrong with him?!! Do good for people and look at what you get. I wasn't mad at the world. Just him. That back stabbing snake! I felt like slapping him in the face!!

Now what do we do? Here we go again. John and I were in the middle of planning the notion of realizing having our baby girl and this happens.

I had to stand on an unemployment line for the first time in my life!! I was disgusted at Richie for doing this to me, to my faimly, and to the business. He needed me there. He was so wrong about this.

Things were very tight financially for awhile. I felt depressed even though I knew it wasn't my fault. I just wanted what I was entitled to. Ooooh, he made me see red!! Look at the thanks I get for flourishing his business. Richie should be ashamed of himself! He knew I had a family!! How could anyone be this cold? That bastard!!

By then, I was used to making such good money. We had to scale back and make cuts where necessary. We used to go out on Friday nights as a family to dinners or a movie and now we had to give that up to conserve money. We ended up having to sell back one of our cars, because we could no longer afford the two car payments. We had to let go of our credit cards and ultimately filing for bankruptcy, because we were afraid to lose the house.

Things were upside down financially. I was shocked that I went from managing a business to the unemployment line. Proof positive that things can change in an instant. So, I prayed even more than I ever had before and asked God to lead me to better days. It was really getting to me and I felt like I was losing it.

There were other issues clouding my mind, too. Shawn was becoming a teenager and trying to find himself as well. He was starting to get into trouble in school. He was getting suspended every other week. I was puzzled and I couldn't figure out why Shawn was being rebellious and acting out like this.

After all I had done to give him a good and secure life, what was bothering him? What was troubling him? I set out to find out. So, I took him to counselors and even went as far as to enter him into The Scared Straight Program. I was on a mission to help him in any way I could. I was determined to get to the bottom of it.

I had been putting in a lot of applications for jobs trying my best to find something as soon as possible. I stayed by the phone praying for it to ring. It finally did. Out of the blue, on a beautiful Spring May day, I heard the sweetest voice on the other end. It was Sofia. Sofia and I had always joked that we should start our own company and to hell with Richie.

She calmly said, "Lala, I heard what happened and I am so sorry to hear you lost your job. I have an idea." The phone went quiet for at least thirty seconds and then she continued, "remember when we said we should start our own company? Well, let's do it!" I replied, "what? Are you sure, Sofia? I know we joked about it, but doing it is something else all together. I don't have the money to partner with you."

To which she quickly responded, "that's okay, Lala. You have the knowledge and I have the money. Money plus knowledge together equals partnership and a successful business. What do you say, Lala?" I was speechless. All these thoughts raced through my mind. Where do we start?

The very next day Sofia and I met for dinner to discuss this new business opportunity. She brought along her new husband, Morty. Morty began the conversation by asking me, "Lala, how much money would you need to get started and how long would it take to start receiving money back in the business?" I took a second to think and then pieced it together.

"Morty, we're going to need at least $100,000.00 to $150,000.00 to start. I already had done my homework and came up with those figures from the research I had previously done. I even factored in reserved payroll for two months in case it took that long for facilities to start repaying us. I told him we would also need money for liability, general, professional, and worker's compensation insurances along with office furniture and equipment.

At first, Sofia was taken aback, because she said, "Oh, goodness, Lala, I didn't know we'd need to start with that much." I assured her that that was the funds we'd need to make it until companies started paying us.

Sofia sat quiet for a moment trying to absorb my figures and realized I was right. She then looked at me sincerely and said, "ok, Lala. I don't have all that money, but I have a sister who loves in Paris. She owns a restaurant. She knows what I want to do and has agreed to help me." Before I could respond, Morty chimed in with a very firm voice, "why would you borrow anything from anybody, but me? I am your husband. I will help you out. Sofia, I will give you the money to do this."

Sofia was so happy to hear of his generous offer that she responded, "Morty, are you sure? Would you like to be a partner?" He laughed and said lovingly, "Sofia, no I don't want to be directly involved. You know I'm a doctor and don't have the time to be dedicated to this. This is yours and Lala's project. You both can handle this."

Sofia pressed on, "Morty, if you are going to give us the money for this and you don't want to be a partner, then I will pay you back for every cent you're lending us." He chuckled and retorted with, "You don't have to pay me back, honey. I am your husband and I want to everything you want and need." Sofia was on cloud nine with this wide grin on her face. I have never seen her that happy to the point of utter content. It was set.

By this time, John was no longer working at the hotel. He had gone on and found another job as a forklift operator, which gave him a pretty good salary. Our two sons, John Jr. and J.J., were now on the Reisterstown Mustangs Football Team. John and I, along with his parents, excitedly went to every game. They loved football. Shawn was trying out for all different sports. He could never stick to anything long enough. I still had him attending counseling.

A few weeks later, Sofia and I set out to find our new office. We found it in Pikesville, Maryland. It wasn't much. Just three hundred square feet of space. We ran to buy furniture and set up the office. We were so elated that everything was now coming together. The very first month, I was in high gear, and procured ten contracts! I had placed an ad in the local paper requesting RN's, LPN's, and CNA's. I knew from managing Richie's office that we had more than enough employees.

We were booming!! I ran the business and now had two assistants working for me. Sofia couldn't do too much. She was pregnant at the time. So, I told her, "Sofia, take it easy. I can handle everything. Concentrate on having the baby and I'll take care of everything on this end."

Sofia took my advice and then also decided to go on vacation with her husband Morty to New York City. It just so happened to be the week of September 11, 2001. I was at work in Baltimore when I heard on the radio that The Twin Towers were hit by two airplanes! There was speculation that terrorists were involved. People were heard saying that Allah had made the terrorist kill all those innocent people. I was petrified for Sofia, because she is a Muslim and Morty happened to have the same name as one of the accused terrorist!

Morty is not religious at all. As a doctor, all he ever believed in was science. I desperately tried calling the hotel where Sofia and her husband were staying, but there was no answer. I hung up the phone and cried. I prayed she was all right. I kept thinking about her baby. It made me feel so distraught and helpless that I couldn't do anything, because I was so far away.

Finally the phone rang. It was Sofia and she was crying hysterically!! She screamed, "Lala, did you hear what happened?! They have Morty and me locked in a room at the airport questioning us as if we were terrorists. As if we had something to do with taking the towers down?! They had the nerve to ask us if we were Muslims and why are we here in N.Y.C. They checked all of our bags and strip searched us! I can't believe this is happening to us! What a way to start our vacation!!"

I just listened in shock and amazement. I couldn't believe what they were going through. It was like a nightmare that I wasn't waking up from. I called John and told him everything and he was in shock, too.

After several days of hell in N.Y.C., Sofia and Morty decided to end their trip and fly home three days shy of their vacation. The next couple of weeks weren't any easier for them. Television News Reporters surrounded her house on a daily basis. She and Morty were constantly receiving prank phone calls all night every night. They were going through absolute hell.

I was so worried for Sofia especially because she was pregnant. This had taken a toll on her. She was normally very vibrant, playful and full of life. Seeing Sofia pregnant delighted me, because she always said she wasn't going to be the one having any kids and now look at her! Never say never!!

I remember a funny experience we had had in the office awhile back. One of the employees had come in with her baby and the baby threw up on Sofia!! Sofia just kept saying, "ill, ill, ill." Her facial expressions were so funny. I never laughed so hard. Thinking back, she must love Morty a lot to change her mind about having kids.

Given the aftermath of the terrorists attacks, Sofia couldn't even really celebrate the joy of her pregnancy. She was highly stressed out. She worked herself to death. She was staying at the office until 11:00pm at night to avoid reporters camping out at her house.

One day, Sofia went to her regularly scheduled doctor's appointment. The doctor delivered her the most devastating news. Sofia's baby had died inside of her. There was no heart beat. She believed it was due to the stress she was under. Sofia called me and asked me to meet her at a restaurant, because she wanted to talk to me. It was raining heavy that day and I wasn't sure what she wanted to tell me. So, I was nervous and anxious to speak with her.

Chapter Six
Tragedy and Triumph...

I reached the restaurant first. Sofia arrived about ten minutes later. I was beside myself. What was the news? Was the baby okay? Was the business going to be closed? Was she getting divorced? Did her husband get arrested or have another woman? It was driving me nuts!!

When she saw me, I was still in the car. It had been raining so hard that I didn't want to come out until she got there. She looked lost. She was walking toward me in the rain and she got soaked. I was afraid to get out of the car based on her approach. But, my emotions overpowered me and I jumped out of the car to see what the hell was going on. She didn't have an umbrella. I could tell she had been crying. Her eyes were swollen.

I asked her, "what's wrong, Sofia, what's wrong?!" She grabbed me and hugged me and then whispered, "Lala, the baby has no heart beat. My baby died." I was crushed. We both began to cry in the rain and got drenched, but we didn't care. We were grieving the loss of her child. She and I were truly devastated.

We were outside in the rain so long that drivers were stopping in their cars to ask if we were all right or needed any help. I was absolutely stunned. That wasn't the news I was expecting. My heart dropped down into the pit of my stomach for her. Of all the things I have been through in my life, I would put that day as one of the worse. That such a tragic thing happened to someone that was so dear to me.

I thought we were going to be celebrating the birth of her child. I wanted to be the baby's Godmother. She explained to me that she had been under way too much stress and that had a profound affect on the baby. I barely had any words to say. I just kept thinking why oh why, Lord, why? Why the baby?

Sofia and I grew even closer and closer as friends, sisters, and business partners. We shared everything in our lives. Her home life started to decline due to Morty's job as a physician. He was staying out all night after work drinking his sorrows away about the baby and about Sofia and their lack of communication.

Sofia felt no support from Morty, so she turned to me and we ended up spending more and more time together. She would often invite John, myself, and the boys over for dinner so that she would have company. She also introduced me to her extended family and they accepted me with open arms.

Six months later, Sofia got pregnant again!! This time, because of what happened before, her doctor put her on bed rest. I would go to her house every single day and make sure she had food or anything else she needed. I took her to all of her OB/GYN doctor appointments. Morty was still out of control. He was afraid she'd lose the baby again. He was just a mess. On the other hand, John was so supportive of what I was doing and said, "Lala, I have the boys with me and Sofia doesn't have anyone. Stay with her as much as you can and give her the support she needs."

That made me love John even more. He was a blessing and so loving and truly considerate. Morty, unthinkingly decided to move out of their bedroom and leave her alone. He actually moved down to the basement of their three story house!! Sofia ignored him. She ended up hiring a housekeeper to come in twice a week to clean up after her and Morty. Poor lady, she had to clean up stacks of dirty dishes and trays overflowing with cigarette butts from Morty.

Sofia and Morty had a lot of communication problems in their fragile marriage. In their culture and customs, the women sat home, had babies, and never second-guessed their husbands. Whatever the husband said, went. Sofia wasn't that type of woman. She was the total opposite. She was very outgoing, independent, and wanted nothing more than to have her own business and make her own money.

Not exactly what Morty was used to or comfortable with. She never covered her hair like the traditional Muslim women and wore American women business clothes. She was born into the Muslim faith and once explained to me, "Lala, just because I don't cover myself up like they do, doesn't mean that I don't believe in God." She also said, "Muslim women cover themselves as a sign of respect. They chose not to show their skin to anyone else but their husbands."

I decided to ask her to explain to me the difference between her faith as a Muslim and mine as a Christian. She gently said to me, "Lala, people have it all wrong. We have the same God. God is God and He is all by Himself. The difference is we don't believe that Jesus is the son of God. We believe Jesus is a prophet. Just like Muhammed and the rest of the prophets. God is a loving God. No God that loves his people would want them to hurt themselves or anyone else. So, when you hear people saying that I am doing this in the name of Allah, meaning God, that's hogwash! Those people are sick and really brainwashed by other sick people."

She went on to say, "it's no different than when Jim Jones convinced Christian followers that God wanted them to take their lives." I then told Sofia, "I don't think that people really understand the Muslim religion." My family and I have met her whole family. I even got to spend time with them in Morocco. While there, strangers came up to me and kissed me to death. I was so moved by that!!

Her family fed me more than I could ever eat. Their generosity was endearing. I visited and prayed at their Mosque, which is their church. I felt so welcomed and loved. It was amazing to me how many people came out to pray on a daily basis. I learned a lot from that experience and it told me to never judge a book by its cover no matter what other people say. I used to be so ignorant about other cultures until Sofia opened my eyes and she really changed my life and how I see things.

Things were taking a toll on Sofia with all the reports camping out in front of her house still. Strange phone calls, harassing people, and others who were just jumping to the wrong conclusions. She was trying to stay calm, because she was almost due to have her baby. She was petrified of a repeat of what happened to her first baby, so she was doing her best to keep her cool.

I decided to throw her a special baby shower at a restaurant and take her away from all the drama. I surprised her and chose the very same restaurant that she had first worked as a waitress when she came to America. I broke tradition and had invited Morty and their other mutual friends along with our friends and co-workers.

Unfortunately, Morty nor his friends ever showed up for the shower! That pissed me off. Sofia was clearly hurt, although she tried to play it down. No one picked up on it, but, I knew. I could read her face. We got through the shower even with the tension present. She received really beautiful gifts from all of us and said, "thanks everyone, I really appreciate you guys."

Sofia had had enough. The next week, she moved into a hotel. She was disgusted with Morty. She felt so tired of him ignoring her needs. Not to mention all the hormonal changes she was feeling from the pregnancy. After about a month at the hotel, Sofia decided to go looking for a house. She didn't want her first baby to be born or living in a hotel. She said to me, "Lala, I guess Morty will have his house and I'll have mine."

You could tell she was disappointed that her marriage was pretty much over. So, to give her the utmost support, I accompanied her to the closing of the house she had purchased. I was happy for her to finally be moving on, but I was also sad, because I knew this isn't the way she wanted it to be.

Sofia's trials of life took a toll on me as well. I was going nuts helping her, trying to manage my own house, and being a wife and mother. Not to mention running the business, too. I could tell that in the back of Sofia's mind that she wanted Morty and her to work things out. Who could blame her? No one wants their life to fall apart.

That Summer of 2003, Sofia delivered a beautiful, healthy, gorgeous baby boy, whom she named Jack. Sofia said, "it feels bittersweet without Morty here." He came to the hospital after he was born. You would think that a father would go to the hospital to see his wife give birth to their son, my God. Bring them a card, a teddy bear, flowers, or something! He came empty handed!! He didn't even ask her if she was ok and if everything went all right. He just held Jack in his arms for a bit and then he left.

Surprisingly, a year later, Morty sued her for sole custody of Jack, although he had never been there during her whole prenatal care and delivery. Sofia blew her top and filed for divorce immediately. She was livid. She'd cry a lot, but would allow him to see her suffering. Rightfully so. He didn't deserve to know.

Before all this turmoil ensued, Sofia and Morty had bought a house in Florida, because the plan was to open up another branch of our nursing agency there. I had already built a multi-million dollar company in Baltimore and we had placed a manager to run the day-to-day operations. I was extremely excited, because I had gotten all thirty contracts for the hospitals in Baltimore by myself!

John and I along with our boys drove down to Florida in February to find a new house. We were elated. Things were really looking up. It was getting better and better for me and my family. I no longer had to pinch pennies and count every dollar I spent at the grocery store or in the mall.

Things were improving in Dee's situation as well. Marc had proposed and finally married Dee. So, I didn't have to worry about her as much. She was more secure now and I was thrilled about that. I still had my issues with Marc, but now that he married Dee, I was cooling down on him.

I never in my wildest dreams thought that I would be living in a thirty-four-hundred-square-foot house with a pool in a cul-de-sac!! When I was little, I was always told that I'd end up like my mother and have nothing in my life, which played in my head over and over as I went through my new house.

I was so determined not to let that happen to me or my new family. I had prayed on that a lot and God had granted me my wish. He had sent me Shawn, then John, then Jason, and now Sofia, who was like my new guardian angel. I didn't have a college degree in business management, but what I did have was the experience and the drive for success. I knew the nursing like the back of my hand. All I ever needed was for someone to believe in me and Sofia certainly did. I just loved her.

I moved to Florida in June 2003. I worked, did all of the collections for our Baltimore company five days a week, and began to settle in our new strikingly beautiful home. Sofia decided to sell the home she had bought with Morty in Florida, because of her impending divorce. Shockingly, the plans for the new office in Florida had to be put on hold, because Morty, who originally wanted nothing to do with business, now was being a hard ass and claimed he was a partner through his monetary investment and wanted half!!!

Sofia had already paid him back every penny he had invested, so how could he now be entitled to half?! I could actually count on one hand how many times he even visited our business. He even made jokes about the business thinking it wouldn't succeed. But, Sofia and I defied the odds and had a very strong and flourishing business now. It was very demanding and stressful at times, but we always said, "yes, it's hard, but it's worth it, because it's ours!!"

It wasn't easy for us. There were times we had to go and pick up payments from our clients just to make payroll. We never even borrowed any more money from Morty. We wanted to prove that we could do this on our own with God's blessing. How could Morty be so unfair? How could he take part of our business? How could a court reward him with half of our hard work?

I found out through the divorce proceedings that Sofia was forced by Morty to exclude me as a partner! My name wasn't on anything! So, in the divorce settlement I received nothing! Sofia privately offered me $25,000.00 when she sold the business, which was quite noble of her.

This was actually the second multi-million dollar company I started and I ended up with very little. I should have learned from my previous mistakes and protected myself from what Morty was able to do to me. I had trusted him too much and thought he knew what he was doing. But, now I saw that he was protecting himself instead of me. Why had he not protected both of us at the same time?

All I could do at that moment was pray for the best. One of my church members asked me, "what did you learn from all this experience, Lala?" The sad truth was that I learned that I can't trust people. Man will always change, but God always remains the same. He has forever been by my side and I know He never failed me. Morty may have won the battle, but with God by my side, I intended to win the war.

After Sofia's divorce was final, she entrusted me to open the Florida office called Quality Health Professionals. I still had a sore spot for the way Morty burned me before, so this time I did the paperwork and protected myself. Sofia and I were made as equal partners. John decided to quit his job and come and work for us. He did all of the billing and helped me with the staffing. Sofia continued to treat me like a sister, but Morty told me to watch my back. He said she was good at hiding things from people and you wouldn't find out until it was too late. At that time, I ignored him and pushed on through.

I kept that in the back of my mind and thought to myself if she is hiding something, I'll find it out one day. We opened the business in

Florida in 2004 and as I knew it would, it grew into another multi-million dollar business! John and I became increasingly financially comfortable. We were now drawing in an annual salary of more than $250,000.00. Life was so good for the next few years. We were so proud of ourselves and we were enjoying the fruits of our labor.

Sofia was still living in Maryland, so I took care of all the day-to-day business tasks in Florida. She was handling all of the company reconciliation and sometimes worked on call. She was able to answer the phone 24/7. I was so glad that what Morty did had caused no damage to our close friendship. We were determined not to let anything come between us.

The previous fall, around October 2003, I received a phone call from my father-in-law, John Sr., telling me that the stock market had crashed and that he and his wife, Gloria, were behind in all of their bills. They were also in danger of losing their home. John Sr. was retired from the telephone company after more than thirty two years of service.

He had served in the Army and was such a nice man. I couldn't believe that they were now going through this. He was the go to guy in the family. He was the baby, but everyone turned to him for help. He would even take us all on family trips. So, I had no idea they were in bad shape. Gloria, my mother-in-law, was very nice, but a shy woman. She was a housekeeper, who decided to keep on working when John Sr. retired. When we had lived in Baltimore, she always invited us over for Sunday dinners. We weren't even permitted to miss her home cooking.

I went to my husband, John, and talked to him about what was happening to his parents. I suggested that his parents move to Florida and live with us. John turned to me and said, "Lala, are you sure?" I told him, "yes honey, I have always wanted to have a big family and I love your parents very much." They had always treated me more like a daughter instead of a daughter-in-law.

So, we called them and asked them to move in with us and they agreed! They were so happy, because they missed us so much. We made arrangements for them to move into our home. After they arrived in Florida, they set out to find full-time jobs right away. Mom found a job at a local hotel and Dad found a job as a Security Officer. Our children were so happy to have their grandparents living with us. They were really close to them since they had spent holidays and every Sunday with them when we lived in Maryland.

The year before I was able to start the business with Sofia in Florida, I sat for more than a year eating and working from home. That really took a toll on my body. I had gained weight. One Friday, we all decided to take a family trip to Universal Studios. We rented a minivan and were on our way. After we arrived, we enjoyed a few water rides, fun activities, and then it was time for the roller coaster.

The lines for the roller coaster ride were long. So, we had stood in that line for more than an hour. It was finally our turn to get on the Incredible Hulk ride. We got in the seats and sat down. I tried to buckle to seat belt, but couldn't. The ride attendants came over and tried to squeeze me in, but the belt wouldn't close and they had to ask me to get off the ride. I was extremely embarrassed.

Everyone was looking at me and my kids were wondering why they asked me to leave. I let them go on the ride and waited for them on the side. When they got off the ride, they came right to me and asked, "mommy, what happened? Why did you get off the ride?" I sadly replied, "Nothing. I felt a little sick and I asked them to let me off." I had never felt so ashamed in all my life.

Ever since I had my first child, I had begun to gain weight and become more and more overweight. That was the day I made up my mind to go through with the gastric bypass surgery I had been considering. After I went through the surgery, I lost more than one hundred pounds in six months. I felt better than I ever had before. I looked great and my confidence had returned.

Meanwhile, my oldest son, Shawn, was going through his own personal issues. He was now a senior in High School. He was extremely polite and soft spoken for his age. He didn't dress like the other kids with baggy jeans. He dressed in an appropriate way. So, the other teenagers would tease him and call him gay. The pressure proved to be too much for Shawn.

Ultimately, Shawn succumbed to the stress. Right after his junior prom, he entered into his senior year. The ridicule caused him to drop out of High School. My sons and I were really close and we all talked about everything. So, when this all happened, I was aware of his troubles.

I felt so helpless. I wanted to march into that school and scold them one by one.

Shawn finally let it all out one day when he just couldn't take it anymore. He was crying when he approached me and said, "Mom, I'm so confused. People are second guessing my sexuality. I love girls from the way they look, how they smell, and just everything about them. So, why do I feel so confused, then? I told him to ignore what people say. I said, "Shawn, just be yourself and love who you love. Period."

I wasn't quite sure which way he wanted to go, but I was one hundred percent in his corner. He knew I had his back on anything and this was no different. I do believe in civil unions. To each their own I always say. Everyone should have a chance at happiness and if someone of the same sex makes you happy, then so be it.

The Bible tells us to be fruitful and multiply. I didn't want to judge him. So, I told him whatever he decided to do, I'd love him no matter what. I also told him, "Shawn, what's wrong with people today is that they spend so much time judging each other instead of loving and accepting each other as God's children. We should let God be the judge and no one else."

Shawn felt better and we hugged and kissed. He looked at me lovingly and said, "Thank you, Mom for being the type of mother you are." He had tears in his eyes, which I wiped away and gave him a kiss. My other two boys were getting older and now attending a Christian Middle School. They both loved football like you wouldn't believe. Real die hard fans. So, it wasn't a surprise when they started playing for The Reisterstown Mustangs.

John and I were desperate to have a little girl. So, we decided to try again. I went through two rounds of IVF. On the second try, it worked, we were pregnant with our little girl! We wanted to ensure that is would be a girl one hundred percent that we did something called "sperm wash" to wash away the male sperms. It was one of the procedures to give us a better chance of having a girl.

We sat in that doctor's office trying to play God. I knew in my heart it wasn't the right thing to do, but we really wanted a girl after three boys. I know we're supposed to accept whatever God gives us, but we wanted to try for a girl so damn bad. We were thrilled to find out that the IVF worked and we were finally going to have the girl we always wanted.

We had gone out on a limb to play God. We knew He is the Alpha and Omega and didn't need any help from a doctor in deciding boy or girl for us. Nonetheless, we scheduled an appointment to have the embryo inplanted in my uterus. I remember that we went on a Tuesday. After the embryo was implanted, I was told to take a couple of weeks off of work, which I did. I hired an assistant to help John in the office. I felt confident in John and knew he wanted me to rest for the baby's sake. He wanted our baby to be safe.

He told me, "Lala, don't worry or stress. We did it. Now, our baby girl is coming." He was so happy and so was I. At that time, since we weren't sure when the invitro would work, John and I decided to also have a surrogate in another state carry the other embryo. We did it at the same time. So, we both now had due dates in October 2007. But, the surrogate's baby girl came a little early in September of 2007. We named her Jordyn. She was perfectly healthy even though she came one month early.

Unfortunately, my fate would be different. Though I was also due in October, our embryo came premature on July 16, 2007. We named her Jasmine. It had cost us more than $20,000.00 for her to be created. Sadly, Jasmine died two hours after she was born. She was only one pound and just too little to save. She was unable to breathe on her own and she was so tiny that the breathing machines couldn't even fit on her. We were so devastated. Our first baby girl was gone.

I can still remember her little whisper of a cry. So dainty and demure. Tiny, yet weak. I had spent two months in the hospital prior to her birth due to complications and being ordered to bed rest. I prayed so much during this time, but I was also constantly worrying about her fate. I finally had to come to terms with it all and said, "God, let your will be done."

God has the power to show you that He is God and He is God all by Himself. The day before Jasmine was to be delivered, the doctors told me that they had to deliver her before it affected my health. I was scared, but I tried to make my peace with the outcome. I said, "God, you gave your only begotten Son so that we may be saved. I am okay. Have your will. Have your way, Father." Then I cried and cried.

During those two months in the hospital, I watched Tyler Perry's "Diary of a Mad Black Woman." I would replay the song that Tamela

Mann sang in the movie, which was "Father Can You Hear Me." I would then ask God for forgiveness of all my sins. I also had my favorite CD by Mary, Mary. I would also replay the song "Can't Give Up Now" over and over to soothe my fragile nerves.

Yet, my heart was prepared, because I had made my peace with God. He let me know that I was going to be okay either way. The morning of my C-Section, John was at work. Since the doctors had already told me that my health was in danger, they didn't want to take a chance, and decided to take her out. When they finally pulled her tiny body out, they tried to hand her to me, but I told them no and turned my head as if I already knew she might not make it.

She whimpered like a kitten. I didn't want to carry the image of her face around me for the rest of my life if she didn't make it. So, I made the heart wrenching decision not to hold her. Now that I look back, I regret it tremendously. She had only lived for two short hours. I couldn't help but wonder if she had been in any pain. Did she know I loved her? All the time before her birth, day after day, I would rub my stomach and tell her I loved her.

By the time John made it to the hospital, Jasmine had stopped breathing. She was gone and John decided not to hold her either. He came over to me, held me in his arms, and we just cried together. Everyone left the room to give us privacy. I looked at John's eyes and he was in as much pain as I was. Our little angel girl was gone. We sobbed and sobbed until we had no more tears left to cry.

The hardest part of dealing with Jasmine's passing was the interns, dietary aides, and housekeepers who kept coming to the room asking me how my baby was doing. I felt like screaming at the top of my lungs for everyone to leave me alone. I felt that the staff should have informed them of her death and not let them ask me such questions. It was too painful to say my baby had died over and over.

I had delivered Jasmine at Jacksonville Memorial Hospital. I wondered why in such a big hospital that they would chose to put me on the same floor with all the new mommies who had just delivered their babies. I would hear their babies cry and I'd walk in the halls and see them holding their babies in their beds and felt even more in pain, because Jasmine didn't make it. They had their babies, but I didn't have mine.

It was only by the grace of God that I made it through those horrible days. I had such a loving husband in John. He came to the hospital every night and stayed with me until I got released from the hospital. They kept sending Social Workers to come and check up on me and see if I wanted to talk about it. I didn't. They even bought me a keepsake box of Jasmine's clothes, footprints, and pictures. I gave the box to John.

They asked me if I wanted to look at the pictures of Jasmine with them and I said no. I told her that I wanted to look at them with my husband John instead. I even told her that I was fine and that God was in control. I told her that I loved my Jasmine very much, but that God loved her more. That's why he took her.

Three days later, on July 19th, my thirty-seventh birthday, they discharged me from the hospital without my baby. I felt so empty handed. So cold as I left the hospital. I didn't want to leave her, but I had to. I turned and looked up at the floor I had been on and whispered, "goodbye Jasmine, Mommy loves you. Sorry I couldn't take you with me. God is going to take good care of you now. I'll miss you forever, my sweet baby girl."

The doctors had given me a prescription for Valium, but I refused to take it. Remember that my mother had died of a drug overdose and I never liked taking any types of drugs, not even over the counter pain relievers, unless I absolutely have to. Two days later, John's thirty eighth birthday, we had the funeral service for Jasmine. Because Jasmine was so tiny, the funeral home recommended that we have her cremated. Sadly and reluctantly, John and I agreed.

Sofia came down to Florida to be with me and attend the funeral services. That was a really hard day for me. That was the first time I really cried since Jasmine passed away. John was trying his best not to cry or show emotion in public. So, he excused himself and went to the men's room after the service and cried out, "why God, why? Why God, why? Why us, God?" After John came back into the Chapel, his eyes were bloodshot. I knew he had been crying a lot. He was just trying to stay strong for me.

Later that night, while we were home, we held each other for a long time and cried it out. We stared at the Urn that had her name and an angel on it and cried some more again. We were trying to make sense of it all. We thought that maybe God was testing our faith and to see how strong we were. We knew, at that time, that our surrogate was still pregnant and not due until October. We didn't want to have any expectations, because it would feel like another death to us if something bad happened.

Oddly, there was a current news story about a surrogate mother that had changed her mind and decided not to give the parents who were waiting for the baby, their baby. The surrogate had had a real change of heart and wanted to keep the baby. So, we were afraid that that might happen to us. So, we chose not to say anything to anyone about the surrogate until we had her in our arms.

The phone rang just two months after the death of our Jasmine and we were told that our second baby girl, Jordyn, was born. She had come a few weeks early, but she was healthy and fine. We were so relieved. She was perfect. John and I rushed over to meet her. We held her as tight as we could. We then made arrangements to pick Jordyn up from the hospital. We were so excited!! She was a gift from God. Thank you, God.

Chapter Seven
Life moves on...

We were in awe of Jordyn. She had my complexion and a mixture of John and I in her face. She had these big soft cheeks that John and I couldn't stop kissing. She had ten beautiful fingers and ten gorgeous toes! She was dainty with these huge brown eyes. Her surrogate mother then handed Jordyn to John and I.

After doting over her for awhile, I asked her surrogate if she wanted to hold her. She did. She kissed Jordyn's tiny little hands and said, "Jordyn, take care of your mommy and daddy, now." Then she handed her to John. She grabbed me and gave me the biggest hug ever and said, "don't worry, Lala. Now you have two angels. One will be with you and one will be forever watching over you." I couldn't hang on and my eyes filled with tears. I looked over at John and his eyes were filled up with tears, too.

As we were getting prepared to leave, she told us to have a good life. We then started calling our family members and telling all of them we were bringing home our new baby girl. They were inquisitive. They wanted to know why we hadn't told them about Jordyn, but we explained to them that we first wanted to make sure everything was okay before we shared the news with the family.

We brought Jordyn home to meet her brothers. We were excited and scared all at the same time. The boys were elated to say the least. They were fawning over their little sister. Between the boys and their grandparents, we had to fight to share time with her. She was certainly the center of attention in our home and we were thrilled to have her. It had been everything John and I always wanted. Now our family was complete.

Yes, I still missed Jasmine. I wished that my two girls could have grown up together. I'd cry when I was alone and mourn her still. I'd hold Jordyn in my arms and lay her on my chest so that I could hear her heart beating next to mine. It was the most serene feeling in the world. I loved it. We'd watch her sleep for hours and fuss over not disturbing her. We became overprotective of her, because of what happened to Jasmine.

We were determined to keep her safe and make sure she was healthy and strong. I didn't even want her to catch a cold or a fever. I'd tell the boys to wash their hands before they came to hold her or play with her. I was going be a better mother to her than my mom was to me. Life was good. Jordyn was growing fast healthy and strong. She had a pair of lungs on her, too!!! The boys were doing really well adjusting to her, though.

I decided it was a good time to return to work part-time. I started working half a day, three times per week, and I'd even bring Jordyn with me. I had a large office with lots of her baby things in it. She'd sit and play in her playpen and enjoy her toys. Every time I looked over at her, I was overjoyed. My life was set. A beautiful husband, three beautiful boys, a beautiful daughter, a beautiful house, and a beautiful job. I was flying high. I finally had it all. I thanked God so many times that I'm sure He got tired of me thanking him!!

We were in absolute bliss for the next few months, until we got some bad news. Aunt Nilsa had passed away from ovarian cancer. We were devastated. She was my favorite aunt and I loved her. She had turned my life around. She had cleaned up her life and stopped drinking and smoking. She really started to treat me like one of her own daughters and as if she were my real mother.

She was calling me regularly and even came down once a year to Florida to spend a week with us. She finally married Willy and he and I made our peace. I told him, "Uncle Willy, I forgive you for everything you ever did to me." He was so remorseful and thanked me for being so kind. Aunt Nilsa was so proud of the woman I had become. She said, "Lala, I always knew you'd make it." That made me feel so good inside.

Not even a week later, a good friend of mine, Jen, who had moved to Florida to be closer to me, died of liver cancer. She had custody of her granddaughter, Kayla. Since Kayla had no where to go, I took her in. She was just entering her teenage years. I thought my house was big enough, but with her added in, it was feeling a little cramped.

John came to talk to me one night about my good heart. He said, "Lala, I know you want to help people, but you can't save the world. You are always trying take care of everybody else, but yourself." I know he was right, but I'm the type of person that when I see a person on the street, I have to help. I just can't turn my back on that. I just can't.

When we went to Maryland for Aunt Nilsa's funeral, as we were driving, I saw a homeless man and told John to stop the car. He did, reluctantly. I got out of the car, walked over to the man, and handed him twenty dollars. He actually looked at me and expressed, "miss, I don't have change of a twenty." I told him that I didn't want change. I just wanted him to take care and told him, "God bless you." He turned to me and locked eyes with me and told me that he'd never forget me.

That melted my heart. That I made a difference in his life that day. When I got in the car, John yelled at me, "why did you give that man twenty dollars, Lala!! How do you know that he wasn't faking it?" I told John, "how do you know that he is faking? You don't know when God is testing you, John. God has blessed us so many times and we should bless others. What if you were standing out in the cold and needed help like him? You would want people to help you wouldn't you, John?" He agreed.

He fell silent and didn't utter another word about it and I knew even though he felt hesitant about it, he appreciated that I did it anyway. John's heart is as big as mine. He just has a hard time admitting it publicly. I know my husband well and he would have never pulled the car over if he was truly opposed to it. Shh, don't tell him I said that!!

Later that year, we noticed that the business was starting to get slow. We had wanted to expand the business for awhile and decided to move the business further into South Florida, where it was busier. John and I went down to Miami to find a new house.

John and I got on it right away, because we didn't want to lose the business. We found a six-bedroom, three-bathroom, and two-car garage home with a pool on the lake of a gated community! The house had been valued at $1,000,000.00. However, due to the economy and the decline in home sales, the builders were going out of business. It was a fully furnished model unit home that was going for less than half price at $400,000.00. We jumped on it right away and put down a deposit.

After several months of going through the buying process, it was finally moving in day!

We had now had our other home up for sale for more than a year. Unfortunately, after we had moved and also moved the business, it continued to decline. I was now in financial distress. It was getting harder and harder to make two house payments and meet the commitments to the rest of the double utility bills. Since I was now an owner, it was difficult to pay myself and meet payroll. I was forced to rely on my 401k plan and use that to cover all my bills, which upset me to no end.

I had to lay John off due to lack of business! That killed me!! He tried to apply to Walmart and McDonalds, but no one was hiring due to the economy. After we ran out of money, we both were forced to apply for unemployment. I was so depressed. Here we go again with a tough financial drought. I was embarrassed, because I had never applied for unemployment in my life! Now we'd both have to apply!! That was such a shock for both of us. It was a drastic change.

We were used to having a comfortable life, but now that was about to change. Unemployment only paid each of us $275.00 per week. At that time, we had about $10,000.00 in bill expenses per month!! There was no way we were going to make it. What were we going to do now?! I was forced to stop paying the mortgage on our first house, which by the way, was on the market now for two years!

We also had to surrender one of our precious trucks. It was terrible like someone had pulled the rug right from under us. It just couldn't get any worse. We were over our heads in debt and drowning fast. I was so preoccupied with everything that I didn't even hear the door bell ring. Then it rang again. Who's that? I'm not in the mood right now to receive company. What now?

I went to the door and saw a man standing there. I didn't recognize him and thought it might be a bill collector. I didn't want to answer the door, but he was persistent. So, I finally opened the door and asked him what he wanted. He was so nice and told me he was there to sell me a Kirby Vacuum Cleaner! I was like oh my God! Not now. I told him that I wasn't interested in buying anything. As a matter of fact, I felt like asking him if he saw anything in the house I could sell him!!

Surprised at my response, he laughed. The man even begged me to let him do the demonstration so that he could at least get the credit for stopping by. So, I reluctantly agreed. Oh, hell, whatever!!

I knew how hard it had been for me, so I can just imagine how hard it is to go door to door to sell vacuums in this poor economy. Told you my heart was big, right? After the man, who was named Matthew, by the way, showed me his demonstration, we sat and talked for about an hour. I told him that I couldn't afford the vacuum, because I was severely behind in my mortgage and truck payments.

Surprisingly, he stated, "I filed for bankruptcy earlier this year. My wife and I are renting an apartment and I have a broken down car." Gosh, I thought I was doing bad! Geez! I told him that I had an idea and said, "Matthew, if you could catch up on your debts, I could let you take over my house and truck payments." He stood there shocked with his mouth open. It took him a minute to respond with, "Lala, are you sure? Why would you do something so kind for a stranger? I have never had someone that would do such a thing."

I told him, "Matthew, well, now you have and that's how I am. Generous. So, what do you say? It would help me and it would help you." We had a deal. I told Matthew that I believed in Karma. That old adage of what goes around comes around. If I can help someone out as well as helping myself, then it was a win, win situation. He agreed. Besides, I was desperate to solve this dilemma.

Believe it or not, even though I was struggling, I still would send a $100.00 donation to the Jacksonville City Rescue Mission to help feed the homeless for the Thanksgiving Holiday. I just couldn't see people going hungry, especially during the holidays. It says in the bible that "God blesses us with things for us not to be greedy, but to share with our brothers and sisters." I believe wholeheartedly in that. All these things we accumulate are material things. There's nothing more valuable than giving.

Life is too short and when we leave this Earth, we will not take any of it with us. At all the funerals that I've ever attended, I've yet to see a house, a car, or an ATM machine following behind the hearse. Not once. So, I believe in always paying it forward.

Despite this new arrangement with Matthew, money was still incredibly tight. We continued to fall behind in our new house bills and I fell into an even deeper depression.

Sadly, I began to take it out on John and the kids. I was very short with them about everything. I was fussing and fighting with them all the time. I was getting on their nerves and they were getting on mine! There were days that I didn't even have the energy to get out of bed. I'd call John over and ask him to make something easy for dinner for the kids to eat, lock my door, and just cry as I laid in my bed.

I kept asking God why this was happening to me again. I started to think bad thoughts of taking my own life. I had some pills that the doctor had prescribed for me from before for my depression. I contemplated taking the entire bottle of pills and then just going to sleep. So, I grabbed my Bible in desperation and said, "God, what do you want me to do?" I also didn't want my kids or John to come into the room and find me dead from an overdose

I was so conflicted. I remember how I felt when my mother took her life when I was only fifteen years old. I was told that she was found lying on the bathroom floor. I am so grateful that I was not there to see her like that. That would have been horrible. So, for days, I locked myself in the room and refused to come out. John told me that foreclosure notices were coming in regularly now and then we received a notice that our health insurance was cancelled. Great, no health insurance, too!

We were now a family of six and I had a lot of health problems to deal with like severe high blood pressure. What in the world were we going to do without health insurance? How was I going to pay for any of our medications? I just wanted it all to end, for me to stop hurting like this, and for the stress to go away.

One night, at my lowest point, I kissed my children and told them that I loved them very much and that I didn't want them to end up like me. A hot mess! I grabbed Jordyn and put her on the bed with me. I started to cry. All the memories of the fight John and I went through to bring her into fruition flooded my thoughts. I held her little face in my hands and said, " Jordyn, baby, mommy loves you so much." She responded right away very loudly with, "I love you, too mommy. Don't cry, mommy."

As if God was yelling it right through her! We had brought this little girl into the world and now I was giving up. I was still making the payments for the IVF to have her. I was thinking to myself that I had messed up her life. What was I going to do, if I can't even take care of her? What if I lose the house? What if I can't find a job?

My mind was racing out of control and I was having difficulty keeping up with it. I was beyond distraught at this point, I was suicidal. I laid next to Jordyn until she fell asleep. John was still in the office filing out job applications. The boys were in bed and my in-laws were already asleep. Now it was my chance to end it all. So, I got up grabbed the bottle of pills and the Bible, and locked myself in the closet. I read a few verses of the Bible and asked God to forgive me. I was over the edge.

I knew it was a sin to take my life, but I figured if I died, John and the kids would get my $500,000.00 life insurance policy. I came out of the closet with tears in my eyes and went to our safe. I took out the insurance papers and started reading the conditions of the policy. Oh God, it said if the policy holder took their own life, then the policy claim would not be paid! I can't even kill myself in peace!

What a defeating purpose that would be. I didn't want John and the kids to be alone without any money. So, if I couldn't kill myself, then I was determined to let it be someone else killing me. I was going to have an accident on purpose. Would I go to Heaven if I let someone else do it for me? My thinking was out of control. I wanted out, but I want John and the kids to be secure. I would have to have a better plan of ending my fragile life. There was too much on me. I could no longer breathe.

As time went by and I was still alive, I fell into a dangerous depression. I thought of all kinds of ways to do myself in. The idea that stood out most was a car accident. So, I got into my car, drove for miles, and blasted my favorite CD of music, which was Mary, Mary. I chose to play the song "Still My Child" very, very loud. I drove onto oncoming traffic and stopped my car! Cars were beeping as they raced toward me.

I started to pray as I now began to cry hard. As the cars came closer, I closed my eyes, unbuckled my seatbelt and waited to be smashed by numerous cars. I think I blacked out, because the next thing that I remember was a man tapping on my car window asking me, "miss, are you all right? Do you need my help?" When he saw my face, he realized that I had been crying a lot and that I wasn't in my right mind.

He stayed calm and asked me to unlock the car door. I noticed that there were like twenty cars passing around me. Why didn't any of them hit me? Why was I still alive? Why didn't it work? I was in shock and disbelief. The man pulled me out of the car and walked me across the street to the gas station. He then went and got the car and drove it over to where he placed me. He must have thought I was nuts!

He asked me gently, "ma'am, what's wrong? What are you doing?" I began to let it all out. I told him about the enormous pressure I was feeling and how many family members were relying on me. That I was only one person and that it was too much on me. That I just couldn't take it anymore. That I was going out of my mind trying to balance it all. That I needed to just check out and let the pain of it all go.

The man pulled the hair away from my eyes and said, "you are so beautiful and I'm sure you have so much to live for." He told me about what God had delivered him from and some of the difficult things he had overcome. He then asked me to pray with him as he took my hands in his. I began to cry and said, "God, please forgive me. I'm so sorry, God. I just couldn't handle the load anymore. Please take this pain away."

By this time, the police showed up. I guess one of the people from those oncoming traffic cars had called the police on me. The cop approached us and asked me what was going on. The man I was with answered with, "nothing officer, everything is okay here." The cop then asked me, "ma'am, are you okay?" I whispered to him, "yes, I'm fine, but I just need to sit here for a moment."

The man that helped me out then walked me to my car. He hugged me and told me not to give up. He said, "tough times never last, but tough people do." He further told me that my husband and kids need me and I must be strong for them. He added, "this is a test of faith. That God loves me and was testing to see how strong I was." I thanked him for everything and then left. I sat in my car alone for about an hour before I was able to drive. When I finally did start to drive, I looked in the rear view mirror and saw that my eyes were beet red. I was such a hot mess.

I didn't want my family to know what I had just done. So, I drove around for awhile. I stopped at a pizzeria and picked up pizza for dinner. When I reached home, everyone was worried about me. They were asking me where I had been. I lied terribly. I told them that I had gone window shopping at the mall. My hands were still shaking.

It was a tough few days for me to readjust to things. One day, the phone rang and it was a telemarketer trying to sell me a vacation package. As he began to speak, he told me that his name was Joe. I turned the flame down low on the food I had been cooking and walked into the living room. His voice was so calm and soothing, that I just unloaded to this perfect stranger all that I had just done. We must have talked for more than an hour!

He was silent and listened intently. Then, it was his turn. He told me that he was retired from the military and that his marriage had failed. He was struggling to pay her child support and was doing this job just to make ends meet. We bonded. Joe made me promise over and over that I would never hurt myself again. Boy, I could tell he was in the military, because he was yelling these demands at me as if he knew me for years!

He'd say, "Lala, I can't hear you! Say it again! Girl, your husband and kids need and love you! I can feel the passion in your heart, Lala. I can tell that, deep down, you're really a strong black woman. You have been in hard times before and overcome all of those obstacles. God is getting ready to give you something better. Hold on. Don't you give up now!!"

Before he hung up, he said, "God bless you, Lala and I will certainly keep you in my prayers." I thanked him for listening to me and told him I would keep him in my prayers as well. We sometimes need other people to pray for us as much as we pray for others. Things didn't look any better for my family or myself. Unemployment was running out for both John and I. We still couldn't find jobs and the foreclosure proceedings were underway.

Our bank had denied us the Making Homes Affordable plan, telling us that we didn't qualify because we were on unemployment! Ugh!!! For the first time in our lives, we had to apply for welfare and food stamps. Because we were still receiving the unemployment, welfare said we were making too much and didn't qualify!! I don't understand this system? You work hard to pay your taxes and when you need help, you can't get it! Great. So, we'll just starve then.

I had started taking deep breaths and then something amazing came to me.

Sometimes in life you have to humble yourself in order to find yourself. I was determined not to give up now. I realized that there was no easy way out. I would have to see this thing through like everybody else. If it had been meant for me to die, then I would have died a long time ago. I finally accepted that this had been a test. I knew that God had brought me too far to leave me now and now I so wanted to live! Amen!!

I truly love my family with all my heart and I love God so much. I was at a low point and feeling helpless and the devil was trying his best to break me, but God wouldn't let him!! This was the most despair that I have ever felt, but God always makes a way. Amen!! We often lose sight of what's important, God, ourselves, our family, and our friends. I think it was so important for me to finally get that and start giving back.

I have always been so good at caring for others that's why I went into the nursing field. I just wasn't doing a good enough job caring for myself. I had taken care of Dee, my mother, other relatives, and my friends. I was so accustomed to caring for them that I forgot about myself. It happens to the best of us. We lose ourselves in the mix.

There's a great quote by Baltasar Gracien that says, "do not belong so wholly to others, that you do not belong to yourself." Wow, that is so, so true and that's exactly what I was guilty of. Sofia always said to me, "Lala, you have a heart made of gold." I knew she was right. It's just that my heart is so big, y'all, you know.

We get so wrapped up in the day-to-day activites of life that we often put ourselves on the back burner. When we know good and well we should come first as the head of our lives and our households. **Life is a gift and it is selfish to think otherwise.** I had realized that there were also so many people worse off than I was and here I was complaining as if I had a right. I thank God for making me see that He never left my side. He just wanted to test my faith to see if I was the kind of person that He wanted to serve him.

I decided to take the initiative and help those in need free of charge. I knew many people were facing foreclosure and that some of them didn't know what to do. I have great communication skills, so I contacted banks and acted as their consultants. I felt so good helping others again, even if I wasn't quite ready to help myself. I was working on me, though. One breath at a time. One crisis at a time.

The very first couple I helped out of foreclosure was a Mexican couple, who had difficulty with English. I called their mortgage company and made arrangements for a plan that would have reasonable monthly payments. It worked!! They were no longer in danger of losing their precious home and were very grateful to me.

Three months later, two days before Thanksgiving Day, Sofia called me to tell me that she had come up with a really great idea. I was quite curious, so I asked her eagerly, "Sofia, what are you talking about?!" She paused and then replied, "Lala, I want to sign over all of the shares of the business over to you! You'd do much better on your own, since you're running the Florida business practically by yourself." I was in shock. After a few moments of silence, I asked her, "Sofia, are you sure you want to do that?" I knew she had been going through a lot. Her mother had just passed away the week before, her sister had to have immediate open heart surgery, and she was having challenges in her own personal life.

Sofia was facing so much and I didn't want to add any more stress to her life. I had been so grateful for all she had done for John and I. She said she felt good about this and that I should accept her offer. So, I did. She contacted her lawyer right away and told her to start the paperwork to transfer everything over to me. She actually sold me the whole company for one dollar! Sofia always came to my rescue. She even told me that she had been thinking about doing this for over a month!

Sofia said that God put it in her heart to do this. I also think she wanted to make up for what Morty had done to me in the first business. Though I knew it wasn't her fault, she still felt bad about it. I was puzzled and asked her, "Sofia, what about you? How will you make it without the business? She said, "I found a nursing job at a hospital in Texas."

I was so happy about getting the business, because I had never owned a business of my own. I was also afraid, because I didn't have Sofia as a crutch anymore. No one to lean on now and no lines of credit. Everything before was in Sofia's name, but she reassured me that she would guide me through and be there for me, no matter what.

My eyes filled with tears and I told Sofia that I loved her so much and what she has meant to me and my family. She lovingly said, "I love you, too, Sis." I remembered what Morty had warned me about before and that I should never trust her, but he was wrong. She had been more of a guardian angel to me than anybody else. She had never hurt me. By the time I had met Sofia, I had my mind made up that I couldn't trust anybody, but she changed my mind. She proved Morty wrong and I was happy about that.

Sofia made me love her and trust her beyond measure. To me, she had a giving and pure heart. She even offered to co-sign for me to buy another house in case I had any trouble making that transition. She told me, "Lala, you'll never have to worry and as long as I'm here, you'll never be homeless." That was reassuring, because I was doing as much as I could on my own.

She told me that she was doing that, because I had such a good heart and was always helping other people. So, she felt compelled to do all she could for me. Since Sofia had turned over the shares to me, the business tripled initially. But, then there was a downslide again and I was unable to afford myself a paycheck. I was so far in the hole that I didn't think I'd be able to pay myself for at least a year. So, I had no choice but to start searching for a job.

I had been running the businesses with Sofia for more than twelve years, so I was rusty as far as working for someone else. With all of my medical and nursing backround, I decided to go and sit for the NRCMA(Nationally Registered Certified Medical Assistant). I passed that test with a 92% and realized that after all of those years, I still have my nursing knowledge skills. I then started applying for jobs everywhere I could.

After discussing it with John, I had finally decided that I really didn't want the business all alone. I owed more than what the business was worth. I know that Sofia was trying to help me by letting me have it, but it proved to be too much for me. John and I decided to sell it. So, we put it up for sale.

Sofia was now working at the hospital and I was still trying to find work. Meanwhile, I was still running the business until it could be sold. I was running on empty, because, I had to be available 24/7 in person and via phone. It was taking a toll on me. Still, I believed that God was exercising His master plan. I am living proof that if you give your heart and soul to God and surrender, He will make a way for you.

Though I had given it my best, my heart really wasn't in the business anymore. It had run its course. I was tired and discouraged all at the same damn time! But, my personal life was perfect. I felt like I had evolved into a better wife, mother, and friend. John never gave up on me. He was my rock! He let me cry on his shoulder whenever I needed to and never complained about my stress.

I learned how to pay attention more to my family needs and became a better listener. I was making improvements in my soul, my mind, and my body. I will always trust in God and how He leads me. I know He will take care of me. For He is good all the time not just sometimes.

I was also preoccupied with my father coming home from prison. He now had his only son that was graduating from high school and about to attend college. I was praying hard that dad wouldn't miss that. I always had this dream of becoming an actress. It just kept burning a flame in my spirit, you know. I couldn't shake it, so I had to invest in it. I had to explore this avenue with all my heart and try to see where it would lead me.

I decided to go for it. It was time to stop dreaming about it and make it my reality. I was so driven, it excited me. John had just found a full-time job operating heavy machinery, which was the type of work he previously did before he came to work for Sofia and I. On the weekends, he was still working for me free of charge. He said there was no way he would abandon me. No way. I love that man! Lord, thank you for giving John to me!!

I went after the acting fervently and completed two student films as well as landing a contract for my first featured role!! What God has for me is for me!! We must be grateful and thankful even when we are being ferociously tested. Everything and I mean everything happens for a reason. Now, I know that I was never alone. God was there the whole time. I just had to get in line. Get in line with my mind, my spirit, my soul, and my body. After not seeing a paycheck for many months, now money started coming in. Thank you Jesus! The dry spell was over and I was so proud of us for pulling through our darkest and lowest days. I felt healed and like the financial weight had lifted.

Chapter Eight
Reflections…

The death of Jasmine was weighing heavy on my mind. Every time I looked at her Urn with that gorgeous little angel praying on her knees, I'd cry. Why hadn't I held her in my arms? It wasn't her fault what happened. Yet, I was so distraught that I thought holding her, at that time, would have made things worse. Today, I just wish I would have held her at least once.

I had to make my peace with this, so I took her Urn, got on my knees, asked her to forgive me and cried until I fell asleep. When I awoke, I had the Urn close to my chest. John came in and helped me up. He softly said, "Lala, please don't feel bad. She's with God now." His words resonated in my spirit, but I couldn't respond. My heart was hurting too much.

I pushed myself to get through the day. As I did, other memories flooded my mind. The year after Jasmine died, the hospital contacted me and told me that they were organizing a "Memory Walk" for all of the babies that were lost the previous year and Jasmine was included in the names. At first, I didn't want to go. I thought it would make me feel even worse, but I reconsidered after I spoke to John and his parents.

They all felt that it would help us heal and it would pay homage to her memory. We decided to make a family day of it. We were all going. We were going to represent Jasmine with all of our hearts. On the day of the memory walk, I woke up in a very positive mood. We all got ready and headed to the park where the memory walk was being held.

I was holding John's hand and looked into his eyes. He was quietly letting go of a few tears. So, I held his hand tighter and whispered, "John, she's here with us. I can feel her. She's smiling, because she knows we love her and we'll never let her be forgotten." He smiled at me, but didn't say a word. He needed time to let his tears go. So, I didn't say another word. We came up to the table that we had to register at and were met by a hospital staffer.

She gave us small pieces of paper, pencils, and some purple balloons. She said, "write something to Jasmine and fold the paper to fit into the balloon." So, we did. Each of us stepped away to get some space and think of what we wanted to write. I decided to write, "I love you, Jasmine. You have my heart forever." It felt so good to write those words. I wanted her to know that I would feel her in my heart always.

We started walking to the part of the park that every one had to gather at to unite our balloons. A representative from the hospital said a few words. Then he told us all to raise our balloons, say what we wanted, and then release the purple balloons into the air. I screamed out, "I love you, Jasmine!!" John followed with, "We miss you, Jasmine!!" John Sr. yelled, "I love you, sweet heart!!" The boys were concentrated on the balloons going higher and higher and Jordyn didn't want to let her balloon go!!

We all walked back to the car and got in. We began to talk about how important what we just did was and how Jasmine must be proud that we didn't forget her. That made me feel so good. I was there for her and now I was determined to be there for her forever. I had brought the Urn with us and I held it close to my heart all the way home. Tears were flowing from my eyes and everything I was looking at was blurry. It didn't matter, because Jasmine and I were truly connected even though she was in Heaven and I was here. My soul was more at peace. I whispered, "I love you, Jasmine. I love you."

The car ride back was long and the boys and Jordyn fell asleep. Jordyn had felt bad, because she wanted to keep her balloon, which made me feel like she wanted to hold on to Jasmine. Things got quiet in the car. It gave me a moment to think. I'm not sure why, but I started reflecting back as far as my teenage years. To a time it was most hard for me. I still had not told John about the different arrangements that I had to agree to in order to stay at some of my friends' parent's homes. Some of my girlfriends had older brothers still living with them.

I had spent three weeks at my friend, Keara's house. She had an older brother named James. The day I came to stay at her house, James kept starring at me like I was a piece of meat! He circled around me like he was measuring up a kill. He smiled at me and said, "you and me, later." At that time, I didn't know what the hell he meant, but that night I found out. James came into my room after I had fallen asleep.

I was awaken by his cold hand on my behind. It startled me, but he quickly put his hand over my mouth and laid me back down. He whispered in my ear, "Lala, don't scream or fight, or I will mess you up." I was so afraid, I froze. He removed my pajamas and my underwear. I silently began to cry. He was caressing my breasts and fondling my private parts. I felt so violated. I was still a virgin and didn't know what he was doing. It seemed so strange and too personal to me.

He was moaning and groaning and then he stuck his hardness into me with such a force that I almost passed out. It hurt so much. He was so rough on me. Stroking me harder and harder until he let out this muzzled scream. I thought to myself, what the hell just happened? Did he just rape me?

He tried to justify his actions by telling me, "what did you think? That you'd be able to stay in my house for free? As long as you're here. You're mine to do what I want with and if you tell anyone, I'll kill you." I ran to the bathroom to clean up. I had blood all along the inside of my thighs high up. I slumped down near the toilet and started crying uncontrollably.

I hated him and every time he came to my room at night, I knew what I had to give him. I was so desperate at the time to stay there, because I didn't have anywhere else to go. I had no choice, but to do what he wanted. He was so disgusting with his smoke breath. I had to sit and take it. Talk about being abused. That was something that I kept to myself for so long. I felt so ashamed to be treated that way.

I decided to find someone else to stay with, because I just couldn't take him anymore. I was about to crack. Keara never knew what her brother had done to me. She was too nice to me and I didn't want her to feel bad or feel like it was her fault.

I went to a school friend, Monica, that I wasn't really close to, but she had a single mom. I thought I'd be safe if there was no man in the house. Monica's mom said yes and I moved in with them the very next day. I told Keara that I was going back to Aunt Nilsa's so she wouldn't know anything. I had to get rid of James.

Monica was more like a nerd. I didn't click with her that much, but it was a place to stay. Her mom, Agnes, was seeing a new guy named Brian. He was tall, good looking, and nice at first. Agnes trusted him too fast with us and would often go to work from 4pm - 12am at night. Brian had two teenage girls in the house to choose from, but he came after me instead.

One night, after Monica fell asleep, he came to my bed. He told me, "Lala, come downstairs. I need to talk to you. I hesitated at first, because of the look in his eyes." I could tell he had been drinking. When we got downstairs, he shoved me down on the couch. He ripped my nightgown off and my panties. Oh my God, here we go again!!

I fought back this time, but Brian slapped me hard in the face and told me to stop. I was so shocked that he hit me that hard.

I quickly bit him in the arm and spit in his face. He grabbed me by the throat, lifted me up, and then flipped me over. He held down my hands and head with one arm and used his other hand to pull out his private and shove it into me. It hurt so bad, because he was much bigger than James. I was biting the couch pillow and trying to shake my head loose, but he was too strong.

I could smell his nasty liquor breath every time he came close to me. He did it to me for much longer than James had done. Since I was turned onto my stomach, I couldn't break loose. He kept grinding for more than fifteen minutes. Then he muttered his satisfaction. He laid on top of me for a few minutes and then got up. He told me, "I just couldn't resist. Your body was calling my name." I was furious. I saw that I had left a bite mark on his arm. I cried myself to sleep. I was really angry and felt lost.

The next morning, I called Aunt Nilsa. Things were too out of control and I needed to get out of Monica's house in a hurry. Aunt Nilsa told me that I could come, but not for long, because Willy was there. I didn't care at this point. I left Monica's without telling her a word and headed back to Aunt Nilsa's.

While I was reflecting, I had fallen asleep in the car. John woke me up when we reached home. I was so surprised to see John's face, because the bad memories were so vivid that I didn't realize where I was. Then, I looked into John's eyes I said, "I love you, thank you for saving me from that life." He smiled and helped me into the house.

I called Dee and told her that I was having trouble letting go of some things and she told me, "Lala, sometimes, it helps to write about it." I decided to write it in a poem. I got a pen and paper and started writing. I remembered how throughout everything that God was there. So, I decided to title my poem "I Was Never Alone" and the words flowed...

"I Was Never Alone"

I grew strong as I faced adversity head on...I stood with my head held high 'til each day was gone...The devil proved to be no match, even to the shadow of my five year old frame...I just refused to let him block my spiritual flame...

I had guts to spare...Because, I knew God was there... See, I was never alone...Even when all you saw was me... For God said, "Lala, you were destined to be." With God as my guide...I felt so alive...

Fueled by my determination, I flourished without fear... For it was God who taught me how to steer...My bright light just kept bouncing around...Yet, God always made sure my feet were planted on the ground...

Sometimes, it was really rough...But, I didn't give in no matter how tough...I moved each obstacle one by one...I wasn't going to stop until I was done...I was never alone throughout my life...God was there to make sure I got it right...

He was the beacon of support triple than anyone else... He was forever present for whatever hand I was dealt...I carried God in the crest of my heart...I was never alone nor apart...My kindness empowered my spiritual walls...I had to answer God's call...

No use in looking back, because I was never alone...I've always had the number to God's phone...As the Angels and I rejoice, dance and shout...The devil had to give up and move out!!!

Though my path was filled with thorns, I remained calm...I knew that it was God that drew the map on my palm...I was never alone yesterday 'til right now...When it comes to God's presence, all I can say is WOW...

I was made for my husband John and he was made just for me...For we are bounded by our hearts, you see... Our children are the bonus to our lives...Together, we thrive...So, if I lost everything today...I'm going to be incredibly grateful anyway...

...For I was never alone...I was never alone...Trust, I was never alone...'Cause God was always there...To that, who else could compare?...I love you God...I love you...

Dee was right. That felt so good to write. I think that I'm going to write this all out, so I can heal. I think I'm going to write the story of my life. Let it all out and maybe it can help somebody else heal, too. That's what I'll do. I began to write. I wrote about all the things that I had gone through, the tough things about my past. All my struggles. As I wrote, it all came out.

It made me cry sometimes, but I continued. I had to. I was healing one word at a time. I purged it all on paper. I have to admit that it was theraputic and a relief. Putting it on paper, made me feel like the load I was carrying on my back was getting lighter.

John and I were unable to sell the business and had to file for bankruptcy. It was inevitable since things had gotten so slow. I was happy, because I didn't want to run the business anymore. I felt discouraged and tired all at the same time. It had taken so much energy out of me and I had lost so much time with my family by giving it so much attention. I was glad to let it go.

Soon after, I found out that Uncle Jim had passed away from cancer. Because of what he had done to me in the past, I couldn't bring myself to go and pay my respects. No one in the family knew about our history and I wanted to keep it that way. So, I just sent my condolences via phone and made an excuse as to why I couldn't be there.

I asked John what he thought and he said, "Lala, you have every right not to go. No one can force you to." I felt better. John always knew how to help me get through anything. I still couldn't find a job, so I continued to accept acting jobs. I actually had gotten an offer to do a one-time appearance on a soap opera, but I turned it down. I didn't want to do a show for one day.

I wanted something more steady. Later on, I found out that the network had decided to give the actress that took the role, twenty five episodes! She even got nominated for an award for her character. I wish I had known! That could have been me!! Yet, I was happy for her. It just meant it wasn't my time yet.

I accepted other roles and pressed on. I honed in on my acting skills. I practiced and practiced until I became so confident that I was auditioning for everything and anything. I wasn't going to miss a good opportunity twice!!

Jordyn was getting so big and all her teeth came in. I noticed that she had my sass. I'd go over to her and ask her for a kiss and she'd say. "maybe later, mommy. Maybe later, ok?!" I was like OMG. Did she just tell me no?!! She's got some nerve, but I couldn't be mad at her, because I saw myself in her. I liked that. It meant that she was going to be a survivor like me and that's exactly what I wanted most. For all my kids to be strong and get through anything.

It bothered me a lot that the business had flopped. I felt as if I had failed somehow. Yet, I knew that there were also elements that were not something I could control. I had tried my best and the rest was up to God. I guess He felt it was time for me to let it go. So, I finally did and all the stress that came with it. John was very supportive.

He kept telling me that it was not my fault. I told him, "John, it's hard for me not take it personal." John looked at me and said, "well, ok, but also see it as a blessing, Lala. You got to experience owning your own business. How many people get a chance to do that?" I realized he was right, but it was still bothering me.

I didn't want to tell other members of my family. I wasn't ready to. I felt it was something only John and I should cope with at the time. John agreed. We handled the failure alone and it made it easier for me to cope with. Deep down, I was grateful for the experience, but I was devastated by the loss.

Meanwhile, we were still having difficulty trying to get a loan modification. The bank we were with turned down our application. We found out later that they had sold our mortgage to another bank, which frustrated the hell out of me. Now, we'd have to start the process all over again.

The new bank was more rigid with the paperwork and though we tried, they turned us down right away. They claimed that since we had limited income, that we didn't qualify for the modification. I decided to check to see what our home was now worth. We were shocked to find out that our $1,000,000.00 home was now only worth $150,000.00! OMG, what a severe drop!! So, even if we wanted to sell it, we wouldn't get much for it.

Besides, we didn't want to lose our beautiful home! We were so settled in and it was the most beautiful home that we had ever lived in. We just didn't want to compromise that. I started to pray hard for an answer. God, there just had to be one! There was so much on our plate. John's parents lived with us, our four children, and ourselves. This was our sanctuary and we weren't about to lose that. No way!!

I remembered that I had made calls for strangers as a good deed for them not to lose there homes, so I decided to become my own advocate and do the very same for us. I called the bank and inquired about the rejection of our application. The woman on the other end of the phone named, Janice, told me,"Ma'am, you don't qualify, simply because you don't have enough debt to income(DOI) to even make the new payments."

Then it hit me! I had another house that I was renting and that was income! She said, "well, you never mentioned that before. Let's start a new application with that income recorded and see what happens." Thank you Jesus!! My rental income was a added in! That was it. That kind deed I did so long ago to let someone rent the house would be my saving grace.

I had blessed someone else and now that blessing was blessing us! She got started on the process right away. I told John the good news and he hugged me so tight. I felt such a relief. I had done for us what I had done for so many other families, saved their home. About a week later, Janice called me. She sounded happy and that was a good sign. She said, "Ma'am, your income now qualifies for a loan modification." I screamed, jumped up and down, and yelled, "thank you, Jesus!" Janice laughed and said, "I guess I made your day!" I came back with, "Janice, yes you did, girl!! Yes, you did!"

A week and half after that, I received a package from the bank of new forms to fill out. I was so excited. John and I filled them out together and sent them all the papers they had asked for. I wanted to send it back as soon as possible before they had a chance to change their minds!! I wasn't wasting any time. I stood in the living room and looked around. We weren't going to have to give up the house! Whewwwwhewwww!!!!

God is amazing, isn't He?!!!! He sure is!!!! Dee called me saying she wanted to come for a visit to Florida and see me. I said yes with enthusiasm! She was like, "girl, you're in a good mood." I said, "yes, Sis, I am!!" She wanted to know why, but I didn't tell her, because she knew nothing about the struggles John and I were in and I wanted to keep it that way. Though we are sisters, I was reluctant to share my deep hardships with her. I felt that she would say I told you so or something and I didn't want to hear that. I was too happy!!! After we hung up, I twirled around the living room like a little girl!!!!

John was working full time now and I still hadn't found a job. My unemployment was about to run out and I was nervous. It felt like I was going to have an anxiety attack. What do I do when the unemployment benefits run out? We can't make it without that money. I decided to step up the search. Many jobs still felt that I was over qualified. I tried to assure them that I had no problem taking a job at entry level, because my benefits were about to run out.

I went to every interview, I kept buying the newspaper to look for jobs, I even went on foot trying to see if businesses had any store signs asking for help. Nothing. I came home tired and so sad, because there was nothing available. I was very aggravated. At that point, I would've taken anything. Hell, even a teenager's job at a fast food restaurant wasn't out of the question for me, but even those were filled!!

OMG, it was like the devil was blocking every step I made. I was fed up and turned to God and said, "God, I'm trying my best. I can't find anything out here. What am I going to do? Please help me. I can't do this without you." I opened my eyes and let out a deep breath. I know He heard me. I just know he did. Something would come up soon.

See, I realized with God, that when we pray, it may not happen exactly when we want it to, but it certainly happens when God wants it to! Believe that!! So, I waited until God opened the door to my next opportunity and I was more than ready.

Two weeks later, the phone rang. There was a bit part in a movie available. The woman on the phone said, "we'd like you to come in and read for this part." I didn't even ask her about the movie, what part it was, or nothing. I just said, "can I have the address of where I have to be." She laughed and said, "but, you didn't even ask me about the part." I quickly stated, "I don't care what it is. I need a job." She gave me the information and I was there the very next day to read for the part.

They liked my personality right way. I read for the part as if my life depended on it, because it did. I got the part!! Shooting started the next week. I felt like a natural at acting. Besides nursing, nothing gave me more satisfaction than acting like I was somebody else. I think it was a great escape. Being someone else for awhile, let me take a break from my reality and I so needed that. I really did.

Don't get me wrong, my home life was great, but the financial stresses were too much. I wish we didn't have to pay for anything. You know, come to think of it, we are the only animals on the planet that have to pay for every damn thing! How come the Lions, elephants, or chimps don't have rent to pay? How come the ant, tiger, and pig eat for free? Don't get me started!!

Every single animal on the planet lives, eats, and sleeps for free!! We are the only stupids paying through the damn nose to survive!! Hell, I wonder what it would be like if the tax man showed up in front of the giraffe and said, "Mr. Giraffe, here's your tax bill for this year." I'm sure the giraffe would kick him in the damn head!! LOL

So, how come we are made to pay until we're damn near broke!! Wish I had their way of life, for real. Wouldn't it be cool to live in your house for free, to get groceries for free, to go out on the town for free?!! Wish we damn could!! Instead we have to come out of our pocket 'til our noses bleed. Can't even get an ice cream without a dollar! Why did I start? OMG!!!

A few weeks went by and John and I had been checking the mail every day looking for our approval letter. The last day of the week for mail, that Saturday, it finally came. Our approval letter was short and sweet. We had been approved for the loan modification and our new payment starting that March would now be over a $1000.00 less!! Wow, thank you God!! We'd be able to afford our mortgage and at least some of our bills. God is amazing!! Thank you, Jesus!!

John Jr. and J.J. were big enough now to offer help and went out getting odds and ends type of jobs to contribute to groceries and some utility bills. We were going to make it. Some how, some way, it was coming back together. We had pulled through, because we stayed united instead of divided and that was key.

John felt a little bad that the boys had to give their little bit of money, but I told him that it would make responsible men out of them. He realized it, too and allowed them to do so.

I had decided to join a computer social network to get my name out there and to see if I could find jobs quicker. I found it to be a good connection and started making friends. People on there were very supportive and kind. There were some men trying to ask me out even though my status said "married." They had some nerve. None of them could match what I had in John. None of them.

Surprisingly, I was getting propositions from females, too! They were even bolder then the men! They sent me racy half nude photos of themselves. Talking about, let's be friends! I was laughing so hard. I'm only into men, baby, and ain't no woman got what I need!! OMG!!! Where they for real?!! OMG!! Yes, they were!!!

Thank God there was an ignore and remove friendship request features! Every time someone got out of line, I'd hit remove friend and bam they were gone! Loved that feature!! No hastle and no fuss. I'd post my acting videos to let people see me in action hoping that a producer or director saw it. It gave me a feeling that I was staying current and allowing my work to be seen.

I always screened the people requesting me as a new friend. I'd go to their info page and see what they were all about and if I didn't like what I saw, I ignored their request. One day, while checking my page, I saw this friend request from someone named "Joelle Valente" and thought that she looked like me. I checked her info and saw that she was a poetic writer and photographer.

Her message to me read, "Hi, Lala. I'm Joelle. Nice to meet you bright spirit." I thought she was kind and she seemed genuine, so I accepted her request. Within a few hours, we were exchanging messages. She thought I was funny and I thought the same about her. She was different in that she was interested in me and not what I do. She asked me about myself, my family, and she told me about herself and her family.

I felt such a connection to her and I could tell she really liked me as well. We soon exchanged phone numbers and heard each other's voices for the first time. She sounded exactly as I had imagined. She was down to earth, light hearted, funny, and positive. Right away, I realized we could talk about anything. She wasn't judgmental or opinionated. She was caring, friendly, and concerned.

We are both sassy yellow chicks!! OMG!! I felt comfortable enough to tell her that now that we were becoming sisters and she agreed. Just like that we bonded. She loved me and I loved her. She felt like family right away. I joked to her that we'd be the new Oprah and Gail. She laughed hard and said, "yes, we already are!" See, right there, I new she was genuine. She really liked me as a person and I really liked her,too.

She told me that she wrote poetry books and did photography and that she was in the middle of writing her second book. Then, a thought came to me. Why don't I ask her to write mine?

We were talking every day now and I felt confident enough to ask her. I said, "Joelle, I know you said you write poetry books, but do you think you could write a book about my life? I already have the outline and all you have to do is follow it." She was quiet for a minute and then said, "Lala, I write poems and take pictures. I've never written a book before. I think you should have a professional do it." I felt that she was trying to guide me to someone else, but deep down I felt like she could do it, even though she thought she couldn't. I had a strong feeling inside that she could.

I left it alone for a few months and then decided to ask her again. This time, her first book was completed and on it's way for sale. She had started her second book the month before and she was telling me about it. I told her, "Joelle, I know you said that I'd be better off with a professional writer, but I like the way you write and express yourself in your poems and that's what I'm looking for."

This time, she didn't hesistate. She said, "ok Lala, send me the outline you have and I'll get started on your book." Thank you, Jesus!! I sent it to her e-mail right away. She told me that someone had given her a book for Christmas and she begun reading it. She read five pages of that book and got bored. Then when she got the outline I had sent her, she said she read through the night and couldn't put my book outline down! Amen!!!

Joelle was so excited about my story that she started writing my book right away. She loved the title "I Was Never Alone" and she said, "Lala, this is something really special. Your story must be told. It would be an honor for me to write this book for you." I hung up the phone and thanked God for her. See, God is instrumental in every single blessing we have. Don't ever forget that!!

Joelle and I began to talk more frequently and not just about the book, but our lives. She shared things with me and I shared things about my life with her. We kept saying to each other that we were meant to find each other. She surprised me one day and told me she was going to revise the dedication of her book to include me! Wow, that felt awesome.

While she was busy writing my book, she mailed me her book called "The Valente Parables" Volume I and as she had promised, on page three of her dedication, it read:

To: Mrs. Lashawn Butler...My new Spiritual Sister and Dearest Friend...God was instrumental in tying our hearts together at both ends...You and I were meant to find each other...I know we will always be there for one another...xoxo...☺

I felt so touched by her gesture and my heart smiled. I knew I had found my new best friend. She didn't even give me a chance to call her. When she thought the book should have arrived, she called me and asked me, "Lala, did you see the dedication?!"

I told her I did and I thanked her.

Chapter Nine
Life Falls Into Place...

I was so excited that Joelle was working on the story of my life. Every time she completed a chapter, she'd e-mail to me so that I could read it. Though I had written an outline for her, I was emotional when I read how she put it together. I called her one night close to midnight. I knew I could call her at any time.

Another idea had come to me. So, I said, "Sis, I think that my story should be made into a movie as well." She immediately agreed. I told her that there were so many lessons and struggles to my life, that maybe it would help someone get through if they knew what I had made it through. She listened intently to me and then replied, "Lala, I'm going to talk to the publishing company that put out my poetry books and ask the owner if she knows of anyone." We spoke about a few other things and said good night.

I fell asleep with a smile on my face and that wondrous thought in my mind. That week, Joelle called the owner as she had said she would. Then, she called me with such an eagerness in her voice, "Lala!! The owner of the publishing company told me she has a playwright contact on standby when your book is complete!!!" All I could say to Joelle was, "thank you, Jesus. Thank you, Jesus!!"

I knew we were really on to something truly special. Our new friendship, the book, and the movie!! God, I love you. Joelle and I bonded more than sisters, in my opinion and I just kept thanking God for her over and over.

Joelle and I were leaving each other messages on our computer pages that we loved each other. We were talking to each other's daughters. Her daughter, Maris, who has special needs, always gets so excited when I call. She feels the bond between Joelle and I and embraced me, too. My little Jordyn gets on the phone with Maris all the time and they get a kick out of talking to each other. They're a riot together!!

Joelle has always been so optimistic and always inspired me to get through my tough times. One day, while I was telling her about my financial struggles, she cleverly segwayed into asking me for my bank account number. She said she had a few extra dollars and would send it to me so that I could pay some overdue bills. She called me once she made the deposit.

I asked her, "Sis, what did you do? How much money did you send me?" She said, "Lala, I'm not telling you. Go check your account and call me back." When I went to check how much she had put in, I was shocked to see that she had generously made a deposit of $5000.00!! I couldn't believe it. I wanted to return it to her right away, but she said no. God had sent me an angel. She even told me that I didn't have to pay it back!

She lives in New York and I live in Florida, but that day, I felt like running from my house to hers and hugging her with all my might!! She had just done the most unselfish thing anyone has ever done for me! How could someone love me so much right away like that? She made me cry right there, but they were such happy tears.

Joelle and I grew even closer. She opened her heart and I opened mine. It was so easy for us to confide in each other. For many months, she had been my rock. Until one really emotional night, when I would now be hers. She has such a positive personality that I wasn't ready for what she unloaded on me.

That night, she called me, she had been crying hysterically. I thought she had been hurt or something horrible happened to her! She said, "Lala, I just read a horrible story in a gossip magazine. A little ten year old girl had been found dead, raped and killed by her adoptive father in Florida." I had heard that story on the news and knew who she was referring to. The little girl had been found dead in a plastic bag in the back of the adoptive fathers' truck.

Joelle was crying so hard that I had to calm her down so we could talk about this story. I had never heard her like this, so I was in shock. She was inconsolable for a few minutes. She said, "I can't take it anymore, Lala. We have to do something about this."

She felt that these innocent children were crying out to her through that little girl who was killed. She was so deeply affected by her. So we began to talk.

Joelle decided to tell me about her childhood. She had grown up in twelve different foster homes and had been abandoned by her mother at the age of five! She said that she had been sexually molested by seven of those fathers that lived in different homes. She said she was always afraid to tell someone. The fear overwhelmed her at the time. I could tell that her emotions were really high. She was that little girl who desperately wanted someone to hear her voice, but didn't.

Then it hit me! The little girl in Joelle was crying out to me along with the little girl in Florida that had been killed and I was going to help them both along with the little girl inside of me that had made that cry no one heard. I calmed Joelle down by telling her that we needed to gather ourselves and come up with a way to help all the little voices out there that need to be heard.

I told Joelle, "why don't we start a charity that would lend a helping hand to all those little fearful voices?" Her sentiment changed almost immediately. She quieted down and then said, "Lala, that's a great idea." I told her that we can form a non-profit organization that would give strength behind those little voices like never before. Now, we were really onto something. Since I already had business experience and Joelle had writing experience, we'd unite those blessings and form our charity.

We needed to come up with a name first. I came up with "Voices of Angels" and Joelle came up with "Angel Voices" a clear indication that we were on the same page. Joelle felt so strongly about "Angel Voices" that I felt it was important enough to her to go with that name. So, now, we had a name for our charity. Joelle had stopped crying and I was broken hearted to have heard her cry like that!!

I never wanted to hear her cry like that again and I was determined to see this charity through. I knew more about business than Joelle did and I explained the ins and outs with her. We were going to make this happen for all those little angel voices that wanted to be heard. On Monday, I contacted the name search division for registration to make sure no one else had the name and got the ball rolling. I wrote down all the steps I needed to make and get the charity up and operating. I knew that Joelle and I were meant to do this. It would be our calling in life to help all the little girls and boys out there that were afraid to use their voices or just didn't know how. We were going to be their lifeline.

We were excited that we had figured all that out in one talk. It was meant to be. Joelle felt reassured and we began to move in a positive direction. I was also doing this for Jasmine. For her little voice, too. She was my spiritual angel and I wasn't going to ever let her down. She gave me more strength every time I thought of her. I had written a poem to her and I read it over and over to the point I have it memorized...

"Our Baby Jasmine"

Sweet, Baby, Angel of ours...You've now become a Heavenly Flower... To watch over all of us as only you can...We just know God's holding your hand...You took your journey right away...We're so sorry that you didn't get to stay...

We love you more than you will ever know...Swear we see you in the night stars that glow...I've still got your little hand in mine...A promise I make 'til the end of time...

Your brothers and sister love you, too...Your grandparents are still talking about you...I can still remember all your little tender kicks in my womb...I imagine you sharing Jordyn's room...

I know God's got you by his side...We can feel it in all the tears we've cried... We needed our hearts to express just this...You are surely missed...You will always be our daughter and our first princess...We still have your mementos like your first dress...

So, weep for us not and rest your head on the clouds...As we cheer you on and express that we're so proud...Proud that you came through us...We were sad when you had board God's bus...

We'll be on our way to meet you, one by one…You stay strong, Baby Girl, as we draw our strength from the Sun…Your life may have been short, but our bond and love were not…We will forever include you in all we've got…We love You…So, please keep your sweet love shining through…xoxo…☺

Reflecting back on my good times, especially when I wasn't so worried about counting every dime, a funny story comes to mind. Sofia and I used to go out all the time when we were running the business. We were on cloud nine. We walked into this posh restaurant and sat down to have lunch.

Sofia ordered a Seafood Salad and I ordered a chicken sandwich. We had lighthearted conversation and were laughing until the damn bill came!! The waitress handed me the bill and I told her right away, "excuse me, miss, there's been some kind of mistake. This bill says $240.00!!" She said, "no. The bill is right." I almost fell off my chair!!

The Seafood Salad was $200.00!! The chicken sandwich was $20.00!! Then she said, "then, there's the tax!" I bust out laughing like I had walked into the twilight zone!! OMG!!! Are they crazy?!!! I stood up, helped Sofia pay the bill, because, at first, Sofia said she'd be treating. I just couldn't let her pay a lunch bill that expensive. We walked out of there so pissed off!!!

By the time we got to the car, we were laughing again. Thank God, at the time we could afford it. Had it been now, I would have been in the kitchen washing dishes for real!!! LOL!!! Those memories keep me going and understanding that any type of hardship is so temporary. I have to master not fretting over the temporary B.S., you know. 'Cause it just isn't worth the stress that comes with it!!! It gives me such a headache, which I don't need!!

John and I had begun to buckle under the financial pressures. I was snapping at him and he was snapping back at me. It was taking a toll on our marriage and that scared me. We weren't being as intimate as we used to and I withdrew. Oh hell, I withdrew a lot!! I was definitely on edge. The kids were like, "mommy, you are trippin'!!" I snapped back at them, but had to admit that they were right.

I had to give myself a reality check. So, I did. I began to lock myself in my room and pray hard and if anyone disturbed me, I'd scream out that I wanted to be alone. Leave me alone. It helped to have that down time so that I could regroup my thoughts and calm down. I realized that I was taking on too much of the load. I needed to delegate some of it to my family members instead of taking it all on by myself.

My only dilemma was that they just didn't do it like me with the same gumption that I did. That's why I'd be like, "okay, I'll do it myself!" That was my fault, because I didn't have the patience to wait for them to do it my way. I couldn't help it, I wanted it done my way. Something I was going to have to work on if I was to have some damn piece of mind!! Ok, I'm not perfect, but hell, neither is anyone else!!!

John saw a change in me. I wasn't enthusiastic about sex and he'd be calm, but stern about it. I know that we were neglecting each other's needs, but I was in distress. I just couldn't commit to it if my heart was so weighed down with all this crap. The mortgage, the credit cards, the car payments, class pictures for the kids, and the new fall school clothes now were needed. My head was spinning like crazy!

What the hell happened?!! One day I had $100,000.00 in the bank and now, because of all the debt we had, that was all gone. I called to check my balance one day and found it was negative $543.00!!! OMG!!! I just couldn't take it anymore!!! I slammed my bedroom door and got on my knees again for the umpteenth time!! This time, I was more direct with God…

"Ok God, what's going on here?! I had a business, money, and a beautiful house to show for it all and now you take it all away. What gives, God? Huh? What are you trying to tell me now?!! I did everything you asked of me. I worked hard, got married, had children, and owned a business with Sofia. What did I miss?Huh? What did I miss?!"

He didn't answer just then, but I was determined to find out. I started to tackle one problem at a time, one kid at a time, and John's needs one at a time. I figured, since I was trying to juggle too much, I'd lighten the load. If the laundry had to be done, I'd call on John Jr. If the dishes had to be done, I'd call on Jason. Even little Jordyn now had chores!!

She was so cute. She'd pout her lips and act like I was a slave driver. But, if I was to spare myself from a nervous breakdown, something had to give. I was too overwhelmed. I felt so alone at times, yet I had a whole family living with me. So, it was time for them to share in the duties of making things come into balance.

I'd take acting jobs far from home just to leave them there to fend for themselves. I had to. They were too dependent on me and I needed some breathing room. They were suffocating the hell out of me!! I was tired, frustrated, and sad all at the same damn time. It was time for them to step it up. I was too far ahead and they needed to catch up. The funny thing was that they kept blaming me for putting extra on them!! So, I screamed out, "who the hell you think was doing all of this before I gave it to all of you?" Me, me, me, that's who!!!

They looked at me as if I were an alien speaking a foreign language or something! LOL. Yet, I didn't care. It was just too much. I am only one person taking care of the seven people in my household. It was high time they pitched in and took care of me some, you know. I'd talk to Dee and Sofia and they'd agree with me and even tell me, "well, what the hell took you so long?! We thought you'd scream bloody mary long before now!!" Great! Why didn't them heffers tell me sooner?!! OMG!!!!

I had gotten a call to do a guest appearance in a Spanish television series. The acting job called for me to work as a English speaking supervisor of a prestigious hotel for two weeks. The scene was to take place in Manhattan, but we shot it in Florida. It was a good role. Thank God it was in English, because I had so much trouble understanding anything they were saying in Spanish!!!

About a month later, I got a call to audition for a movie called "Time" and it would be a role I was quickly accepted for. They felt I had a natural talent for that part and signed me up right away. I had to pause and call Sharlene Falls, a producer I had met on my social network, to thank her. She was instrumental in me becoming an actress. She had suggested I try out for one of her movies and I laughed saying, "I'm too old now. Ain't nobody gonna want to see me." She came back with, "Lala, a lot of actors were discovered in their forties and fifties and are household names now."

I decided to take her advice and go for it and I'm happy I listened to her. See, God's always right and opens the doors that need to be opened in order for us to be at our best, even when we don't have the confidence to do so at the time. He really does know best. I remember when I was twelve and first started singing in the church choir. Everyone was amazed at my singing voice. They'd always put me in the front to let me lead in song even though I was shy. Again, God making me use my talents.

I was the solo singing act at my sixth grade graduation. By then, I could really blow a tune. They used to say I sounded like the older pop singers out at that time. I got a standing ovation after my song was finished and they were clapping and whistling so hard. Standing up there thinking I was a young Aretha or something! I love singing. It calms me. I haven't done it in awhile, but I'd love to incorporate it into one of my acting roles. So, people could really see how I combine the both together beautifully.

Singing is second nature to me. I'd sing for my grandparents and their friends when I was five. Looking back, I was being showcased and didn't even know it at the time, but they saw something special in me long before I did. I was talking to Joelle on the phone the other night and asked her to go and listen to the message I left on her phone. When she called me back, she was stunned. She was like, "Lala, I didn't know you sang!! Your voice is so beautiful, soft, and so amazing." I was touched, because she's so genuine. She tells me like it is all the time.

She has a fear of flying and I was trying to tell her that it's nothing and she yelled into the phone with, "Lala, are you crazy?!! I don't like flying or big boat rides, ok?!! So, stop trying to convince my yellow behind to get on a plane!!" She had me busting out in laughter!! OMG!!! She's a straight laced Latina with a real street attitude!! I'm not afraid of flying at all. I leave it all up to God!! Hell, if I'm going and it's my time, I'm going!!!! Joelle wasn't feeling that!!! LOL, that's what I love about her!!! She's real and funny, too, just like me!!!

I was reflecting on my twenty year marriage with John and feeling somewhat torn that we allowed so much financial stress to drift us apart. He has always been my very best friend and the greatest love of my life. During these hard times, I could tell he was tired of my sassy mouth. I was pushing him to do more, but deep down I knew he was doing all he could. I thought that if I pushed him harder, he'd feel inspired to get a better paying job.

I was frustrated about finances and I took it out on him a lot. I know he didn't deserve that, but if I didn't let it out somehow, I was going to burst. Joelle and I can about anything, so I called her. She listened without interrupting me and then she said, "Lala, you're upset about the fact that you have less money, but you shouldn't take it out on John. So many women wish they had a husband like John. You'd better go downstairs, apologize to him, and give him a big hug!"

She was right, but I wasn't in the mood to be lovey dovey! I was wondering how the hell I'm going to afford the light bill. She always tries to calm me down when I'm pissed off. She decided to ask me about how long John I had been married. As I was telling her, I mentioned to her that I wanted to renew my wedding vows with John when all these hard times were over.

I told Joelle, "Sis, when I renew my vows, will you be my Maid Of Honor?" She was so touched and said, "yes, Sis, I'd be honored." Then since I knew she didn't like to fly, I told her, "I'm giving your yellow ass a year's notice! So, when the time comes, don't be telling me you're scared to get on the mother fucking plane, bitch!!" She laughed so hard and dropped the phone. She knew I was right, too. Shoot!!! I ain't playing with her!! She better be ready to represent!! LOL

In our first wedding, John and I had to pay for everything ourselves. So, there wasn't much we could afford. So, this time, I want to go all out. I want a Cinderella wedding! Fancy and smancy!!! That's right! After all we've been through, I'm getting the wedding of my dreams!!! And ain't nothing gonna stop me!!!

When I told John what I wanted, he was like, "Ok, Baby, whatever you want just stop stressing my ass about the bills! I've got enough on my back already and I don't want you coming after me all the time with your saucy mouth, ya dig?!!!! I had to admit, he was right. I was trippin' all the damn time now. I was driving him damn near crazy!! I even would send John out to get me food from my favorite take out Mexican food places. Yes, indeed. My son J.J. was funny. He'd say, "mama, are you pregnant or something?!"

" 'Cause, you keep asking for pregnant woman's food," he added. I laughed and then told him, "no, my ass is not pregnant!! Now, go clean up your room, before I throw you out of my damn house for being a slob!!"

I was having trouble keeping up and I felt like I was drowning for taking on so much. The stress, it seemed to have no end. It felt like I was in some tidal wave pool and the devil was the lifeguard and he was just laughing at me!! I was having nightmares, too. They were getting more and more scary each time.

After a long time of trying to fall asleep, I did and began to have one of those nightmares. I dreamt that a huge bulldozer was plowing into the house!! Yes, I did. That bulldozer was so loud, too!! I thought the damn thing was going to cut me in two!! I ran out of the bedroom, screamed for John, and gathered up our kids. The house was being torn apart and there was nothing I could do.

When we reached outside, far enough away, John and I turned around and saw our home in ruins. Our clothes every damn where and the kids were crying about their treasured stuff. I looked at John and fell to the ground crying. He was trying to comfort me and I slapped him!! I told him, "you should have done more!" He stayed quiet for a minute and then slapped me back! He yelled, "you know what, Lala?!! I've done all I can and I'm not going to let you make me feel less of a man!!"

The slap he gave me in the dream, jolted me awake. I turned and looked at John just sleeping in the bed and I shook him awake. I started crying and said, "John, am I being too much of a bitch? Am I? Tell me John, am I?" He was too tired to answer me and turned back over and fell asleep. I got up and went downstairs to the living room. I headed straight for Jasmine's Urn, grabbed it, and laid down on the couch. I fell asleep again and the dream continued!!

John was talking to the bulldozer guys and pleading with them to stop, but they wouldn't! They said they were only doing what their bosses told them to do. We had fallen to far behind and they decided to condemn our house! How could this have happened? When I awoke, I was so happy that it wasn't true! My house was still intact and everyone was still asleep. OMG!!! The stress was playing out in my dreams, too?!!

I had been suffering from imsomnia and anxiousness. I could stay up round the clock. I was only sleeping three to four hours a night. I got so used to it, that if I tried to sleep longer, I couldn't. The damn stress was even creeping into my dreams and making me worry even more now!! Why did I worry so damn much? Why did I let it get to me like this? I was discouraged by it all and it was mounting on me.

That dream about the bulldozer was incredibly significant. I knew that it meant that I was in dire stress. That I'd have to get a handle on my life or it would all just fall apart. I didn't come this far to fail and it was time to fight back.

I decided to start walking some of the stress off. I'd put my sneakers on and tell everyone I was doing it to exercise, but what I really wanted was to exorcise the stress I'd been under. I grabbed my portable CD player with my favorite Mary Mary CD and hit the pavement. Every step eased my stress.

I'd sing along as I walked and imagined how my life would be without all the stress. I envisioned this mirage. I was walking toward my mini mansion. It had all the amenities that I had desired. Marble kitchen counter tops, imported hardwood flooring, pillars in the front door entrance, and a butler at the front door awaiting my bags from a long vacation.

I began to calm and by the time I came back from my walk, I was smiling. Not because that was the reality I wanted, but because it was the reality I deserved. I had come from nothing, built multimillion dollar businesses, and had a beautiful family. If anyone deserved better, it was us. I set out to climb back up that mountain that I had climbed so many times before and this time, no one was going to stop me.

I wanted my dream wedding, my dream house, and my dream life!! That's what I had worked for all my life, so why should I settle for less than God's best?!!! I know God wanted me to be happy and I wanted to be happy, too!! Isn't that what we all want? The chance to be happy without bills stuffed in our throats?!!!

Walking helped me lose another twenty pounds!! Something that I wasn't even paying attention to until I went to put on an outfit for a job interview and the suit was too big!! Whewhewww!! I was elated!! It was time to get some new clothes!! Nothing is more soothing to me than shopping. It helps me relax and takes me away from the every day dull drums that I had become so accustomed to.

Dee had come down for a visit and she and I set out for the mall. Don't you know that when I got there, guys started whistling at me?!!! I was like all right now. Dee turned and looked at me and said, "calm your ass down, don't forget you're married. I was like, "so, I'm married, but I ain't dead. Damn Dee, stop spoiling my fun! They are harmless and none of them approached me, ok?!!" So, there!!

I know I married. I didn't need her to tell me that. She is so sensitive and I'm more lighthearted. I had downloaded some new pics of me and sent them to my page and to Joelle on her phone. She responded right away with a text that read, "Lala, you go girl!!! You look amazing, Sis!!" It felt so good to hear her say that. I was feeling real sexy, too. While I was in the mall, I went to the lingerie store. I bought something really sexy to wear for John in red!!

Dee was rolling her eyes at me. She said, "men don't need that. They'll just rip it off and it's ruined. You're wasting your money." I ignored her.

That night, I made Dee eat her words!!! When John came home and saw me in the bedroom trying on the lingerie, it was on!!!!LOL. He didn't rip anything!!! He made love to me with that lingerie on and I was so glad I had ignored Dee. I remember my Aunt Nilsa telling me once, "men love to see a woman in red. It drives them nuts!" It drove John crazy, he couldn't get enough of me!!

I was like, "whoa, horsey!!!Whoa!!!" He just kept on going like a stallion or something! I was walking funny for two days!!! LOL!!! Our kids were teasing us, too!! The boys were in the den playing video games and making sex noises!! I was embarrassed, but I laughed it off. Atleast their parents were having sex!!LOL. I snapped back with, "how the hell you think y'all little asses got here?!!!"

One day they'll be the parents and they'll understand. Once you have kids, you'd better get it while you can!! That little Jordyn is always sleeping in our bed!! I know she's only three now, but damn. We can't get any privacy these days. The only reason John and I were able to sex that afternoon, was because her little butt was sleeping!!!

Okay?!!! Get it while you can!! I'm just saying, it's hard to get your mack on with little ones running around crying and clinging on to you. And God forbid you lock the damn door!!! They come to the door anyway and start banging hard on the door anyways!!!! No matter how much we try to ignore them, they don't go away!!!LOL.

I was enjoying all of my new clothes and my new shape and hell if I was going to let it go to waste!! I turned into a sexual diva!! John was so exhausted and had trouble keeping up. He accused me of turning into a teenager who made him feel like an old man!! I was laughing at him and joked, "Baby, I'm chasing you. If you're too tired, I'll go chase somebody else!!" He quickly retorted with, "oh, the hell you ain't either!! That cat is mine, all mine!!!! I kissed him and said, "you know that's right!!"

Our kids were used to us talking openly. I never hid anything from my kids. After all, we are their best teachers, as well we should be. I always told my kids to come to me about everything. There was no subject off limits. I wanted them to ask John and I before anyone else. It was our family motto to learn in the home first. It was okay for them to ask their friends how they did it in their homes, but we weren't changing for no damn body.

They knew our value system about life and they respected it. As long as they didn't get foul with it, we kept everything out in the open. Their friends were shocked that we said it like it was and didn't hide anything from them. They'd tell me that their moms would never talk like me. I didn't give a damn. This was our house and our way, damn it!!! And we ain't changing it for no damn body!!!

Chapter Ten...
Daddy's Little Girl...

I don't know what it is about men and their daughters, but it's a precious bond. Though my dad has been in jail for years now, I was still strongly connected to him. When he was out of jail, those few years, he was really there for me when I got married. He was so damn proud to walk me down the aisle. He was really satisfied with John and how my life had come full circle.

We have always been so close. I could tell him anything and he'd give me advice instead of judging me, like so many other family members had done. I adored my dad. It didn't even matter to me that he was in jail, all that mattered was that we were always there for each other. He's my rock. I trust his advice more than anyone elses.

He knows what I've been through and he knows how to go at my family members if he needs to. He comes to my defense no matter what and I love him so much for that. We still write to each other and I keep him up on everything that is going on. I don't ever let him hear me cry, because I don't want him to feel bad that he isn't here with me. I try to keep him strong.

His grandchildren are his pride and joy. He gets a kick out of hearing about their triumps. It makes him feel like he did everything right in that regard and I love to hear his jolly laugh when he talks about them. It makes me feel like he's right here. Like I can reach out and touch him through his voice.

I don't tell him how much I miss him, but he knows I do. He feels it in my voice. I pray that one day he'll be able to come home. He's serving forty to life, but I know God is amazing and miracles happen all the time.

I just know God's heard my prayers. I just know He has. So, I'll leave it in God's hands for He knows best.

His son moved to California after he received a full college scholarship for basketball. He has never contacted Dee or I again. He had become distant when he became a teenager. He mostly stayed to his mother's side of the family. He does stay in touch with our dad, though.

Jordyn has the same type of relationship with John. She can do no wrong in his eyes. So, I'm usually the one disciplining her. She always jumps into his arms when he comes home. She's like his boss. Whatever she wants from him, she gets. If she's at the top of the stairs, she tell him, "daddy, carry me down." And he does.

John's brother, Taye, married a cool chick named, Kalise. We get along so good. She's like a sister to me now. I was even maid of honor at her wedding last May. Unfortunately, after years of trying, she was unable to get pregnant. Miraculously, one of my nurses found out that there was a little girl up for adoption and I helped Kalise apply for that adoption and she was approved to receive the baby, whom she later named Melody.

Melody became the light of Taye's life. She played a big part in filling the void Taye had had at a young age. He had his first baby girl, Tonya, when he was seventeen, but he and his girlfriend broke up and she took the baby to be raised with her family.

Tonya and Taye became closer the older she got and have a great relationship today. Taye even became a first time grandfather to Tonya's baby boy, Tyrell. Who is now three years old.

John and Jordyn are stuck together like glue. I can't even correct her without John stepping in and making sure I'm not too hard on her. She always falls asleep in his lap sleeping leaning on his chest every night. It reminds me of the closeness my dad and I have always had.

I'm so saddened that I am in Florida and my dad's in Maryland. Yet, we find ways to be in touch with each other through mailing letters and talking on the phone.

John and Taye always take the kids to parks and for walks. They love their daddies, just like I have always loved mine. Men play a tremendous role in parenting our children. A father is a hero on Earth to many of us who are privileged to have had one.

It's sad when I see moms who have to struggle to be the mother and the father to their children. And even though that's an enormous challenge, they pull it off none the less. I don't know what I would have done without John by my side. We may joke and tease each other and even get on each other's nerves, but we truly love one another. He is my rock and I am his.

Since I've been on my social network, I tell him that men try to flirt with me and give me their numbers and he chimes right in with, "where are they at?!! Let me talk to them for a minute!!!" I laugh and tell him, "Baby, don't worry, ain't nobody can take me away from you!!" I love that he's still so overprotective after being married all of these years!! That makes me feel so good that he gets jealous and still cares not to let anyone come near his woman.

I still like to keep him on his toes and let him know that I'm a valuable woman. So that he never takes me for granted. I think it's so important to do that especially today, when relationships are being strained by the elements of life and people are giving up quicker and quicker on their relationships. I wonder what's the rush. You're going to just have to deal with another person and their baggage. Either way, you'll have to deal with somebody.

My in-laws still live with John and I. Gloria and John Sr. are a blessing to John and I. I've never met two people that loved me and the kids so much. They have been through it all with us and I thank them from the bottom of my heart for being great parents to all of us. Family is everything to me. Yeah, we have our fights like anyone else, but we stick together!! We don't stay mad at each other for long either, except for John.

John always holds a grudge longer than anyone I know. I'll be like, "John, let's make love in the afternoon." John will look at me, roll his eyes, and say, "don't you remember what you said to me last week?! You told me to go to hell!!" I'll be over here thinking did I say that, and come back with, "I must have just been mad, John. How come you have to hold on to every little damn thing?!!"

Then, here we go again, fighting and discussing it to death. I wish he would just let things go. Hell, I don't even remember what the I wore last week, let alone what I said to him!! I say a lot of things, but I say them in passing and then I let them go. He holds on to them like tid bits to throw back at me later on.

He still didn't answer my question. So I asked him again, "John, Baby, can we make love and not think about all that?!" He couldn't let it go that day. So, I didn't press the issue, because obviously, he was still vexed about what I had said. I dropped the idea of us making love at that moment and then about an hour later, he came to me and said, "ok, I'm ready, but I'm still mad at you." So, I said, "ok, so, come to the bedroom and take it out on me!!!!"LOL

He sure did!!! I should make him mad more often!!!! Just kidding!!!! Not!!! I have never loved anyone the way I love John. I know it's a womanly thing, but I had never had an orgasm with a man until John. Sex just never felt right with my past boyfriends. They'd always rush me through it. John always took his time and made me feel special in that way. I have to admit, you haven't had sex until you've had a real man!!! Whewhewww!!! It's like night and day, y'all!!!

No other man will ever be what John is to me and I fell in love for the first time with John. He made me feel like a real woman and a real wife. For that, I am very grateful. He knows it. I tell him all the time. He smiles big whenever I tell him that. I also knew he was going to be a great father and friend.

God brought him right to me. I had prayed so hard for him, but had never saw him in any other man. Don't tell him, but he's a big teddy bear. He's so protective of us and is the King of our home. I couldn't even imagine being without him. The house smells like him and even looks like him. Jordyn always tells me, "mommy, daddy is so cute. He looks like a hero doll." She's right. I'm blessed to have a good man and I'll never let him go. I love him. I love my children. I love my extended family and I have never stopped loving God.

I knew I loved John already more than anything, but I loved him even more when we first had John Jr. He was so gentle when he held him in his arms. He was crying softly and introducing himself to our son. He said, "hi, John, I'm your father and you're named after me. I promise to always be there for you and love you with all of my heart."

Sorry I got mushy, but I appreciate my blessings. I have to. They are all I have in this world and they mean everything to me. I may fuss and I may fight, but my family, we're very tight!!! My sons talk to me about their relationships with girls and I give it to them straight. Who better than Mama to tell them like it is? They can ask me anything and they know I'll shoot straight from the hip!!

I love Florida! It's the best place I have ever lived in my life! It's warm all year round with semi-cool nights. The houses are magnificently beautiful. You get so much more house for your money down here, too!! I've never wanted to live anywhere else since coming to Florida. Joelle even told me that she'd like to live here one day, too. She told me that New York had just had the worse winter she had ever seen.

They had five major snow storms and all were above twelve to fifteen inches of snow. Forget that!!! I would never want to be shoveling snow in my senior years!! I break my back enough being a mother and a wife!!!LOL

I love to visit other cities and places, but I always come back home to Florida. It's my paradise. My sanctuary. My Heaven on Earth. I've always felt safe here, too. But recently, one of my aunts, Marie, was the victim of a violent death. She had a next door neighbor, who had a son named Jamal. She would always invite them over, because she lived alone and felt lonely.

Jamal had been visiting her for more than ten years there. She treated him like a son. She always told us that he lit up her day. Unfortunately, Jamal had started using drugs and acting out. Aunt Marie tried to steer him in the right direction and he began resenting her. One night, while he was drunk, he tied Aunt Marie to a chair, stuffed a sock in her mouth, and hit her in the head like twenty times with a bat.

He had taken out all his pain and anger out on the woman that had treated him like a son. Go figure. She ultimately succumbed to her head injuries and died that night. We were in shock and dismay. We knew Jamal and his dad and thought they were always so sweet to our aunt. The very child she took under her wing betrayed her. I think he was angry that he didn't have a mom and hated that Aunt Marie was trying to be like a mom.

She must have been so scared. I prayed that night that her Spirit went to Heaven and that God would punish Jamal for what he had done. I found out later that he was sentenced to life in prison without the possibility of parole. I just looked up and said, "thank you, God. Thank you. Please take care of Aunt Marie for us. She's with you now.

I wondered how you could help someone and treat them like your own and they turn on you like that. I felt sorry for her. She was just trying to help a child feel whole. What was so wrong with that? Aunt Marie, God rest your soul and thank you for being the angel you are. I love you and I miss you, too…xoxo…

Our family outings are nothing short of hysterical. Always chaotic and never without drama. Nothing comes close to us!!LOL Jordyn always wants to dress like she's going to a Cinderella Prom. God forbid I just try to put a pair of shorts and a t-shirt on her!! She thinks that whenever she goes out, she's got to get dressed up like I do when I'm going to work or have a job interview.

She always plays dress up in my room. At the age of three, she's a little diva!! She gets my high heel shoes and puts them on. She wobbles around my room and puts her hands on her hips. I'm in trouble with this one!! She thinks she's grown already. The other night, she went into a crying fit, because she couldn't wear a silk dress I had bought for her. The dress is for her to wear to a Church social.

I wanted to try it on her and see if it fit her right. OMG!! She refused to take it off and actually wanted to wear it to a fast food restaurant we were going to. I told her no and she went into a tantrum. Joelle had called me to see how I was doing and I couldn't even hear her, because Jordyn was crying so loud!

I had to tell Joelle that I'd have to call her back, because Jordyn was driving me nuts!! When I hung up, I told her sternly, "Jordyn, mommy only wanted you to try it on, not wear it. Take if off." She went into a hissy fit and threw herself on the floor. I saw my chance and got her out of the dress. Yes, I did!!

Throughout the day to day living, my depression was still on my heels. Creeping up on me and sending me into quiet emotional fits. I tried my best to hide it from my family, but it would come out in my frustration over the little things. They knew I was still battling with it, but I wasn't interested in talking about it. I was just trying to quell it as much as I could. It took God's help, at times, to pull me through.

I never again fell so low as I had once done before, because my faith in God was stronger now. I knew in order to get through it, I'd have to go through it. No more shortcuts and no more free rides either. Now, I knew better. You can't get across the street unless you walk there one step at a time.

Being a woman now, I recognized my past faults. Back then, I'd quit too fast. If it wasn't going my way, I'd lose my patience and start somewhere else. By not finishing anything, I'd fall into a deep depression and think that God had forgotten me, but I was never alone. God never left my side. He was just waiting for me to catch up to him. It took me awhile, but I finally arrived.

I have good days and bad days just like anybody else. I just deal with them better than I used to. Thank God or else I'd still be a mess today. I pray a lot, more than normal, because I need to. It calms me and it helps me stay close to God, where I should be. I can get through anything now with God in my corner.

Dee and I were drifting apart again. Our relationship always ran hot and cold. Never inbetween. She's very sensitive about the things I say to her, but I'm not going to walk on eggshells. She'll ask my opinion about something and then when I give it to her, she gets mad at me. Well, hell, don't ask me if you don't want to know. I can't lie to people. I say exactly what's on my mind. That's just how I am.

So, she'll resist the urge to ask me something, especially when she doesn't want to hear the truth. I can't do it. If we're out trying on clothes and she asks me, "how does this look on me, Lala?" It comes out like, "Dee, you don't have no business trying that on. Go get something else your size." She'll storm out of the dressing room all offended. What the hell did she ask me for?

Anyway, I told her it was better if she didn't ask my opinion if she didn't want to hear it. We left and it was all awkward in the damn car. She was quiet all the way home like I had committed the biggest crime in her life. I decided not to go shopping with her like that anymore. I'd go with her for a bite to eat or visit friends, but shopping, hell no. Not anymore. She was on her own on that one.

Dee started coming down to Florida less and less. We weren't as close as I wanted us to be, but you know what, that's all right. That's God's way of saying just because someone is your "sister, brother, cousin, wife, son, etc…" doesn't mean that they are your friend. Titles don't mean anything to me anymore. Friendships do.

I hadn't heard from Sofia that much either. She was in Texas doing her own thing. So, I didn't even tell her that bothered me, because by this point it didn't. We all move on in different directions. They went their way and I went mine. That's fine. I'm cool doing my own thing.

I was busy with my John, the boys, Jordyn, my in-laws, other family members, friends, and my acting projects. My unemployment benefits finally ran out and I had to step up looking for acting jobs, so I did. I applied for everything and anything, even extras in a movie if I had to. Things were tough on John and I financially, so no job was too small. I was determined to make it out of this long dry spell.

Joelle was a sweetheart. She'd send me money without saying anything to me, now. She'd tell me, "I'm the older sister, so shut up! I'm not listening to you! Talk to me about something else." I felt like God was working through her for me. I had helped so many people in my life and now God was instructing people to help me. What a blessing.

John finally found a job paying twice what he was making before and I told him to take it right away. He did. I was so proud of him, because he had felt discouraged for not finding something for so long. I kept pushing him and pushing him, but John likes to do it on his own. It makes him feel more like a man if he comes through for us than me initiating it. What's the difference? Men...

Thank God I had started getting a few checks from my acting jobs! We were starving and the refrigerator was so bare. I love take out food, but we weren't able to do that as often as we had in the past. I was making macaroni and cheese or spaghetti. I'd have to make hot dogs or hamburgers instead of chicken or shrimp. We made a lot of sacrifices and not just with food.

The boys were borrowing each other's clothes and my girlfriends were sending me things for Jordyn. All in all, we were getting through this. I tried my best not to think about it so it wouldn't upset me. The boys were now old enough to get jobs and pitch in. So, they did, which was a big help.

Even my in-laws would give us whatever they could aside from their own expenses. They were working at jobs that didn't pay the same as they had made in their heydays and still they contributed. They knew how hard it was for us and they wanted to help. So, I decided to write this poem to my family as a memento of our journey and our strength. Here is my tribute called...

"If Today..."

If today God called me home, I wouldn't feel sad... Because of the journey I was privileged to have...To those I didn't get a chance to say goodbye to, well goodbye... Please be happy for me and don't cry...

If today it was my time to go, I wouldn't put up a fight... Because I know I tried my best to do everything right... To those I loved, you were my absolute Sunshine...My true reason for living and my true sublime...

If today I took my last breath, I'd gladly rejoice...Because opting to love was my primary choice...To those that never knew me, you'll find me in the pages of my story, "I Was Never Alone" book...Or in the family photos I took...

If today I was Heaven bound, I wouldn't even frown... Because life was meant for turning frowns upside down... To those I admired, you inspired me to climb much higher...You made me reach for the impossibilities I so desired...

If God said, "Lala, let's go," I wouldn't fight, or beg, or say no...I'd gracefully comply, simply because in this life, I got a chance to fly...I love you guys!!!

My greatest relationship has been with God. We've fought about which direction I should go, but He always won. I went His way. He's much smarter than me and He's been around a lot longer!!LOL...How can I fight with The Almighty Father? As if I could win!! I'd get sassy with God sometimes and act all grown. I'd say, "God, I'm a woman now, ok? I'm going this way." Oddly, He'd never answer me. I just wake up and head in His direction.

See, God may seem like He's moving slow to us, but He's not. He moves at His pace and not ours. So, that's where Jordyn gets her sassiness from, me!!!!LOL...She has my personality copied to a tee!! OMG!!! She's a little me all over again!!!Ha, ha, ha!!! Atleast, I know she'll be all right. God will take care of her just like He did with me. I wonder if she'll give Him as much of a stubborn fight as I did?!!! I'd better warn Him!! What am I talking about?!! He already knows!!!

Poor John, now he's got to contend with the both of us!!! You men don't have it easy. We are always after you for something!! That's what you get for being on the planet with us!!!Ha, ha, ha!!! God must have thought that He couldn't give the planet just to men. He'd throw women into the mix to make it interesting. What would you guys do without us any damn way?!! Y'all know you need us, too!!

Y'all know you would be bored as hell!! We drive you crazy, but you love us, you need us, and you want us!!! Stop fronting!!! I could just hear some of the guys saying, "oh, no we don't!! God should have given y'all your own Island!" Ha, ha, ha!! You would have been boating to our Island just to have one of us!! For real!! You know there ain't nothing more beautiful then us women!! Can I get an Amen?!!!! Amen!!!

We may not think alike, look alike, or even dress alike, but you know damn well we need each other. That's why God gave this planet to both of us men and women!! It's as much ours as it is yours!! Don't act like it's more yours than ours!! It was meant for both of us to share. Ya dig?!!

Apparently, some of you need to be told that!!!LOL…So, I'm telling you!! That's right!! You heard it directly from me!! I'm going to teach Jordyn, too!! We are equal on this Earth and don't you men forget it!! Before a man can breathe, walk, or talk, he spends nine glorious months inside of a woman, so there!!!! Take that!!

I ain't afraid to tell y'all neither. You know I'm right. Recognize and respect your women. We are the Queens of the Earth. I am always angry when I hear that a man abused a woman, hurt a woman, beat a woman, and broke a woman's heart. I have to give praises to my husband John and all the other good men out there that do respect, honor, and love their women as they should. Hallelujah!!! Amen and Amen!!

I need to take this moment to thank John's parents for giving me such a great husband and friend. They did a beautiful job making a man out of their baby boy so that I could have the man in him I have today. I want our sons to be like John when they become men. That's why I always tell them to treat a woman right and to always make her feel like a Queen. Change starts at home and not in the streets.

We must take accountability as parents to mold our children into greatness and not expect the streets or the classroom to do that for us. So, John's parents and my father are my role models to follow and now it's my turn to do the same. I want Jordyn to one day find the kind of man I did in John. The better example you are as a father, the more your daughter will be looking for the kind of man you are.

Daddy's little girls, as we were all so fortunate to be, will become the kind of women that raise our sons to do the same. In my life, I've had many ups and downs, but I stayed far away from that devilish clown. The devil can't reach you if you've got God as your Saviour. No matter how hard he tries to destroy you, God will cast him away like a rag doll. So, keep God close and don't ever let Him go.

I'm always humbled by God's grace. The way He carried me through and dried the tears on my face. Having God in my life saved me from ending it all. Now, I can climb any wall. See, God is omnipresent. There is no place that He does not exist. Thank God for that. It means we all have a chance to come through the darkness into the light. You can go in the right direction instead of the wrong one. Believe that!!

You are not alone either even when you think you are. You must have faith in God in order to prevail. There is no success in this life without His command. Believe that. He can tumble the largest organizations that choose to operate without him. That's why so many Empires fell in history. The taller they were, the harder they fell.

Look at me getting all philosophical on you, but it's true. If there's one thing I've learned, is that you've got to have God in your life. When we die, we don't go to a rich boat or a rich house, we go to Heaven. Where God resides. So, it's best to live your life with faithful eyes. It's made an incredible difference in my life and trust me, it will in yours.

Don't get me wrong, I still get frustrated by finances, but that's just because the devil is always trying to upset me. So, now I pause when it gets to me and tell the devil to leave me the hell alone. It works, too. He's not able to get to me the way he used to and I thank God for that. That fool doesn't deserve our attention any damn way. Everyday, I pray for God to make me stronger, for my patience to reach longer, for my frustrations to subside, and for me to always have my family by my side… Amen.

"Dear God in Heaven, it's me Lala. I wanted to thank You from the bottom of my heart for never leaving me alone and for always reaching for my hand. For teaching me to appreciate what I have and for giving me John, a better man. I still miss Jasmine, but I know she's an angel by my side. Don't blame me for the tears I must cry. Jordyn is a tough cookie. Guess You made sure she would be. John Jr. and J.J. are becoming men. Sometimes, I sneak into the living room just to watch them playing video games in the den.

It makes me feel like they're still my little boys. Watching them play with them video game toys. My in-laws, Gloria and John Sr., are a Godsend. They give me a love that never ends. Dee is far in Maryland, but we still speak. Sometimes, our distance makes my heart weak.

Our struggles are still with us, but I know You're working on it and we are, too. God, I need to thank you for taking care of all of us and I love You. At times, I know I felt like giving up on me and You. But, You grabbed my Spirit, wouldn't let it go, and kept me glued. I know I wasn't an easy child to keep an eye on. Yet, You never said, "I'm gone."

I trust You know best. When do You ever get a rest?!! Your job to watch us all is so grand. I still draw Your name in the sand. So, You see that You're always on my mind. A love, a bond, and a friendship, so true. So, I bow my head and pray to You.

Heavenly Father, keep us close and guide our paths. Until we transform into Your Spiritual Polymaths. Walk us out of the dark. So, that our Soul lights catch Your spark. I am indebted to Your holiness. Thank you for rescuing me from my suicidal distress. You knew better who I'd become. A loving wife and a mother to my daughters and sons.

I must now acknowledge Your plan for me. The joys, the hardships, and the triumphs that would be. I shall no longer stand in Your way. In times of difficulty, I will know to pray. I will take Your wisdom and make it my own. I will respect your wishes and bow at Your thrown.

I am in such awe at what You can do. That's why I tell others to come walk to You. I'm no longer afraid nor live in fear. 'Cause, I know You're standing right here. I now take You everywhere I go, which makes me boast this new spiritual glow.

God, I apologize for giving You such a hard time. It took me awhile to get myself in line. Your faith in me carried me through. So, I'm paying my dues. Walking with my head held high. 'Til You reach for me from

Your Heavenly skies. I see now that I was never alone. That You were in all of my difficult zones.

I was never alone, because You were there. To love me, to give me, and to share. Yes, I was never alone, never was, never had been, never will be...Because You, God, believed in me"…. Love Lala…xoxo…☺